A HISTORY OF

A HISTORY OF
USAFE

Cees Steijger

Airlife
England

Copyright © Cees Steijger 1991

First published in the UK in 1991 by
Airlife Publishing Limited

British Library Cataloguing in Publication Data
Steijger, Cees
   The history of U.S.A.F.E.
   1. United States Air Force. United States Air Forces in
Europe
   I. Title
   358.413520973

ISBN 1 85310 075 7

Printed in Singapore by Kyodo Printing Co. (Singapore) Pte. Ltd.

Airlife Publishing Ltd
101 Longden Road
Shrewsbury SY3 9EB
England

Contents

ACKNOWLEDGEMENTS · · · 6

CHAPTER ONE · · · 9
Portrait of an air force

CHAPTER TWO · · · 25
The European air wars

CHAPTER THREE · · · 53
Peace: jet fighters and atom bombs

CHAPTER FOUR · · · 63
Air aid to Berlin

CHAPTER FIVE · · · 73
The Cold War

CHAPTER SIX · · · 93
The turbulent sixties

CHAPTER SEVEN · · · 115
The USAFE's style of the seventies

CHAPTER EIGHT · · · 143
Into the eighties and onwards

APPENDIX · · · 173
Major USAFE Organizations

INDEX · · · 177

Acknowledgements

My first introduction to the US Air Force dates from 1958, when as a child I was taken by my father to visit the Soesterberg Air Base near our home town of Amersfoort. I can still remember how we both watched the awesome take-offs and landings of the North American F-100 Super Sabre jet fighters then stationed at Soesterberg. This first introduction was impressive and it awoke in me a lasting interest in aviation in general and the American air force in particular.

This interest grew as I listened to my father's stories of World War 2. For a young lad, which I was at the time, such stories are first and foremost 'exciting'. I heard tales about fast Mustangs that flew way up in the sky protecting the mighty Flying Fortresses from German attack. As he spoke I could hear it all; the monotonous drone of the heavy bombers, the thunder of the German artillery, the rattle of the machine-guns; the liberators were in action.

But there was, of course, another side to the war, one which my father did not like talking about. Such as when a Mustang attacked a group of Dutch civilians on a food-finding expedition in the east of the Netherlands. The effects of the attack must have been terrible. My father was in the middle but luckily survived. And there was the time that an American fighter got into difficulties over Amersfoort and ejected both fuel tanks. They just missed my parents' house but caused death and destruction further up the street.

My father's stories were fascinating. I began collecting books about the period. Later I first widened my scope, and my collection, to include World War I and eventually narrowed my focus again and concentrated on the American air force in Europe. I visited museums, collected information, documents, photographs, etc. In short, I was curious about everything that had anything to do with the subject. Out of all that has come this history of the United States Air Forces in Europe. It exists now thanks to my father who regrettably did not live to see how a child's outing to Soesterberg became a man's lifelong interest. And a book.

The inspiration to actually put words on paper came in 1980 when I received the book *The Historical Highlights: USAFE 1945-1980* from Dr. Charles H. Hildreth, Command Historian of the USAFE at Ramstein, Germany. This chronological summary formed, in fact, the basis for this book.

From 1980 onwards I worked systematically researching the backgrounds to the events. I pored over numerous books, reports and articles, corresponded with and interviewed many US Air Force personnel. In particular I would like to thank Dr. Charles H. Hildreth, Dr. Charles O'Connell and Robert T. Cossaboom of the USAFE History Office who provided invaluable information and guided me through the intricacies of American defence bureaucracy. Their assistance enabled me to find the right people in the right departments.

Sometimes it was necessary to verify certain information on the spot and on occasion such visits revealed new facts. A visit to the Regensburg City Library in Germany, for example, threw a totally new light on an incident that took place in March 1953.

I owe a great deal of gratitude to a number of people who have given their assistance without any hesitation. I would particularly like to mention Captain Smiley J. Veal and Sergeant Leslie R. Dortch, both of the Alabama Air National Guard, and Master Sergeant Lawrence A. Weisz of the Missouri Air National Guard who gave me a great deal of 'local' information about the 1961-1962 Berlin Crisis. Sergeant Leslie R. Dortch also brought me in contact with several pilots who were deployed in Europe in 1961 while Master Sergeant Lawrence A. Weisz produced several as yet unpublished evaluation reports concerning the European deployment of the Missouri Air National Guard.

Spontaneous assistance was offered by many people including Lieutenant-Colonel (Ret) James McLennan who, in 1961, experienced a European deployment as a F-86H pilot with the New York Air National Guard (138th TFS). He sent me some magnificent photographs of the 138th TFS's High Flight to their French base.

Getting hold of good photographic material was a time-consuming problem but I did not make it easy for myself by striving for unpublished material whenever possible. It was worth all the difficulties searching through archives in France, Germany, Italy and the US. Most of the photo material comes from the archives of the US Air Force, the US Department of Defense and the Smithsonian Institute in Washington. The photographic departments of the various aircraft manufacturers have also supplied a great deal of usable material and in this context I would like to make special mention of Robert C. Ferguson, Chief Photographer of Lockheed.

Still on the photographic side, I owe aviation photographer Ton van Schaik a great deal and I must also mention that Ton was able to visit and take photographs at many different locations throughout the US thanks to the good offices of Colonel Thomas G. Hanlin of the US DoD Foreign Press.

For his advice, suggestions and photographs I thank aviation journalist Dick van der Aart who read the first draft of the manuscript. Many of his suggestions have now been worked into the finished book, as have those of my colleague Dr. Tom van Koppen, War Historian. He also read the manuscript and advised me on political matters.

And naturally I thank Denise Cooper who translated the Dutch manuscript into English and in the last phase of writing came up with some new and usable ideas. Thank you for a job well done.

Contrary to what appears to be normal practice I would like to mention all the people who have helped in some way or another:

Apple, Lieutenant-Colonel Nick P, Magazines and Books Division USAF, Arlington;

Austin, Major William H, Magazines and Books Division USAF, Arlington;

Berg, Captain James A, Media Relations Division, DoD, Washington;

Bharos, Astrid, US Information Service, The Hague;

Black, Major Donald L, Media Relations Division, TAC, Langley;

Bollman, Ole R, Public Information, Defence Command, Norway, Oslo;

Boucher, Jacqueline R, Media Relations, 50th TFW, Hahn;

Boulet, Colonel J G, Information Service, Department of National Defence, Ottawa;

Brown, Charles A, Public Relations, General Dynamics, San Diego;

Casperini, Colonel Roberto, General Affairs, Italian Air Force, Rome;

Castillo, Technical Sergeant Richard P, Public Affairs Division 27th TFW, Cannon;

Cooper, Ian, writer, Soest;

Cooper, Senior Sergeant Karla L, Public Affairs, 305th ARW, Grissom;

Cox Terrel, Mary Ann, Media Relations, AFRES, Robins;

Crooks, Captain Kerry A, 55th SRW, Offutt;

Diemer, Roberta A, Service Branch, Smithsonian Institution, Washington;

Dilda, Lieutenant-Colonel James H, Media Relations, HQ USAFE, Ramstein;

Dou, Colonel Gilbert, Service Historique de L'Armée de l'Air, Vincennes;

Engel, Barbary, Public Affairs, 108th TFW, McGuire;

Ferguson, Aldon P, Burtonwood Association, Reading;

Flaherty, S D, Public Relations, FR Group, Wimbourne;

Foster, Robert A, McDonnell Douglas Company, St Louis;

Frueling, Captain Todd A, Public Affairs, 9th SRW, Beale;

Gamma, Lynn O, HQ USAF Historical Research Center, Maxwell;

Gann, Harry, Aircraft Information, Douglas Aircraft, Long Beach;

Green, 2nd Lieutenant June B, Magazines and Books Division USAF, Arlington;

Greer, Lieutenant-Colonel James L, Media Relations Division, DoD, Washington;

Grizzle, 1st Lieutenant Sammie C, 7100th Air Base Group, Rhein Main;

Hidding, Ebel, Hilversum;

Isabel, J F, News & Information, General Dynamics, San Diego;

Johnson, Lieutenant-Colonel William H, Media Relations HQ USAFE, Ramstein;

Karayannis, George M, Public Affairs, 381st SMW, McConnell;

Koerts, Henk, aviation photographer, Hoevelaken;

Lash, Fred C, Media Relations, United Technologies, Stratford;

Lawhon, Captain S Dian, chief Public Affairs, 56th TTW, McDill;

Marzinski, Captain Victor L, Public Affairs, 81st TFW, Bentwaters;

Matthews, James K, Command Historian, MAC;

Miller, Masters Sergeant James E, Public Affairs, 52nd TFW, Spangdahlem;

Moscatelli, Major John J, Media Relations Division, TAC, Langley;

Murone, Vincent P, HQ AF Inspection and Safety Center, Norton;

Norris, Geoffrey, European PR, McDonnell Douglas, London;

Paige, Senior Sergeant Ivy, Media Relations, 401st TFW, Torrejon;

Phillips, Major Suzanne L, Public Affairs, HQ MAC, Scott;

Pickering, Brian, Military Aviation Photographs, Lossiemouth;

Roberts III, Captain Sam A, Public Affairs, 36th TFW, Bitburg;

Rodriguez, Norma, *Airman* magazine, Kelly;

Schoenherr, Major M A, German Ministry of Defence, Freiburg;

Sellinger, Sergeant Mary K, Media Relations, 20th TFW, Upper Heyford;

Shellner Jr, Captain Earl, Captain Media Relations, HQ ATC, Randolph;

Sliter, Major Lester A, HQ USAF Historical Research Center, Maxwell;

Solander, Lieutenant-Colonel Eric M, Magazines and Books Division USAF, Arlington;

Spaniel, Bill, Public Information, Lockheed-California, Burbank;

Studio D & S, Hilversum;

Suthard, Pete, Smithsonian Institution, Washington;

Tabak, Marinus D, aviation photographer, Drogeham;

Tizzard, Marion, European PR, McDonnell Douglas, London;

Triestram, A L, Information Directorate, NATO, Brussels;

Trumpp, Dr, Bundesarchiv, Koblenz;

Tucker, Lieutenant-Colonel Charles G, Public Affairs, HQ PACAF, Hickham;

Tuninger, Jan, Information Department, Swedish AF, Stockholm;

Urben, Captain Francis J, HQ Aerospace Audiovisual Service (MAC), Norton;

Weber, Dwight E, Press Relations, General Relations, General Electric, Cincinnati.

Finally, this book would never have been written without the support of my wife, Kitty. It has certainly not been easy for her. In 1986, when the greater part of the manuscript was drafted, I spent every free moment, day in and day out, weekend after weekend and even a good part of the holiday writing. Her encouragement, her understanding and, I must admit, her typing was vital. It is, therefore, to her that I dedicate this work.

Cees Steijger   Leusden, February 1991

The military potential of the balloon was soon discovered. Military balloons were first used by the French Aérostatique Corps.

Chapter 1
Portrait of an air force

The United States Air Force (USAF) officially came into being on 18 September 1947. At least, that is when it became an independent fighting force within the US Department of Defense (DoD). Until this time the USAF — or Aeronautical Division as it was then known — had been a unit of the US Army's Signal Corps. This Army Aeronautical Division had existed since 1 August 1907 when it had been set up as a logical result of the military developments at that time.

Although manned balloon flight was considered a curiosity by the American Army Chiefs of Staff, their French counterparts thought differently and in 1794 the world's first air force — the Corps Aérostatique — was set up. It first saw action on 26 June 1794 during the battle of Fleurie in Belgium when tens of hot air balloons were used for reconnaissance and to provide range and direction information to the artillery batteries. After the battle these balloons were also used to survey the defeated Austrian troops of the Prince of Saxe-Coburg.

American military observers saw the hot air balloon as an ideal platform from which to survey enemy troops and artillery positions from a great height. In addition, it soon became clear that using balloons could improve communications considerably. Indeed, signal flags could be seen from a far greater distance if they were up in the air in a balloon and balloons began to be used in a function now fulfilled by the well known Boeing E-3A AWACS (Airborne Warning and Control System). A modern AWACS unit also operates as a flying observation platform, though nowadays the aircraft are equipped with advanced electronic apparatus and up-to-date radar and can 'see' hundreds of kilometers behind enemy lines while the signal flags of old have been replaced by digitally coded messages transmitted on secret radio frequencies.

The Aeronautical Division

More than sixty years would pass before the balloon and with it (military) aviation was introduced in America. It finally happened during the American Civil War (1861-1865) when the fanatical balloonist John Wise advised the Federal Army to put hot air balloons into action. He had suggested balloons be used for bombardment back in 1846 during the Mexican War but had not been taken seriously. In 1861, he was and a Balloon Corps was established within the Federal Army. The Corps had seven balloons which were primarily used for reconnaissance. The experience gained during the Civil War was extremely useful in the ensuing years. In 1898, for example, a large hot air balloon was used during the Spanish-American War which was fought in and around Cuba. It was only one balloon, but effective nonetheless.

In the same year the US War Department granted Samuel Pierpont Langley a subsidy of $50,000 for his research into a powered aeroplane. Langley had already spent several years on the development of the steam engine-driven aeroplane. His research was supported by Army General Adolphus Greely, Commanding Officer of the Signal Corps, and by the renowned inventor Alexander Graham Bell. At the same time, Charles Manly, a very promising student mechanic from Cornell University, was charged with the development of the petrol engine that was to provide the power for Langley's aircraft. By the autumn of 1903 Langley had completed his work and the first test of his powered aeroplane was held on 7 October. The test did not go as he and his commissioners had hoped: the aeroplane failed to get airborne. Later attempts also failed. During a final attempt on 8 December 1903 Langley's prototype was so badly damaged that it had to be scrapped. The American government, who saw Langley's attempts end in a total fiasco, promptly turned off the subsidy tap.

The irony was that just over a week later, on 17 December 1903, two bicycle makers from Drayton, Ohio — the famous brothers Wilbur and Orville Wright — made the world's first successful powered flight from an airstrip near the town of Kitty Hawk in North Carolina. The US War Department, still perhaps smarting from Langley's failure, were somewhat sceptical of the Wright brothers' success. The possibility of the Wrights supplying their aircraft was not even discussed. The breakthrough did not come until four years after this first successful flight. On 1 August 1907 Brigadier General James Allen signed the order for the formation of the Aeronautical Division within the Signal Corps. From that moment on the American Army had an aviation department responsible for, 'Balloons, air machines and all kindred subjects'.

Above: Brigadier General James Allen founded the Aeronautical Division in 1907. *(US Air Force)*

The greatest air power

Over the following forty years the Aeronautical Division was rechristened respectively the Army Air Service, the Air Corps and the United States Army Air Force (USAAF). During World War 2 the USAAF developed into the biggest air force the world had ever known. In 1944, when it was at its largest, no less than 2.4 million men were responsible for a fleet of nearly 80,000 aircraft. After the war the size of the Army Air Force decreased rapidly and by 1947, when the independent United States Air Force (USAF) was established, there were only 300,000 men and 28,000 aircraft remaining.

With the Korean War the number of personnel increased dramatically until, in 1955, at the height of the Cold War, the USAF once again had at their command more than 28,000 aircraft and nearly a million men. Despite the international crises of later years, such as the Cuban missile crisis, the building of the Berlin Wall and even the Vietnam War, the USAF has never again had more than 900,000 personnel in service and the number of aircraft has decreased steadily. Today the USAF is still the world's largest air force although now it has only around 600,000 personnel. The Chinese Air Force with 490,000 personnel comes second, having overtaken the Russians who, according to the recent estimates, have around 475,000 men.

As far as operational fighters are concerned, the ranking is very different. With its 7,500 combat aircraft

the Soviet Air Force has by far the largest air force fleet in the world. China again takes second place with 5,500 combat aircraft and the USAF with 5,000 combat aircraft (including around 1,730 fighters belonging to the Air Force reserve and the Air National guard — the American National Reserve) comes third.

★ ★ ★

The organization of the USAF

The Air Force Department, like the Army and Navy Departments, falls directly under the US Department of Defense (DoD). The command structure goes via the Secretary of the Air Force and the Air Staff (USAF's Headquarters) to five operational organizations of which the Major Commands, the Air National guard and the Air Force Reserve are the most important. The real core of the USAF is formed by the twelve Major Commands. These include the Tactical Air Command (TAC) and the Strategic Air Command (SAC) which are of similar size, the Military Airlift Command (MAC), the Alaskan Air Command (AAC), the Pacific Air Command (PACAF) and the subject of this book — the United States Air Forces in Europe (USAFE).

★ ★ ★

The Tactical Air Force

The Tactical Air Command (TAC) that is headquartered at Langley Air Force Base, Virginia, is an important air command and is often called the cornerstone of the USAF's mobile strike force.

The core of the TAC is formed by two air forces, the 9th and the 12th, which between them have 24 front line Wings with a total of around 2,000 combat aircraft. The TAC has three main tasks. First, it is responsible for maintaining the front line Wings which, in the event of an international crisis, can be deployed overseas. Second, the TAC provides tactical training for air force personnel stationed in the US, Europe (USAFE) and the Pacific area (PACAF). Although the USAFE and the PACAF are independent Major Commands, they must still be considered as overseas extensions of the TAC. The TAC is also represented in Central America, and operations in both this region and the Caribbean are co-ordinated from the TAC's Southern Air Division Headquarters at Howard Air Force Base near Panama. Last but by no means least, the TAC is charged with defending the United States against hostile air attacks and supplying the US's contributions to the North American Air Defense Command (NORAD). The air defense of CONUS (Continental United States) was formerly the task of the Aerospace Defense Command (ADC), but in 1979 the ADC was dissolved as a Major Command and brought under the command of the TAC.

The TAC's wide-ranging organization also includes the 1st Air Force that comprises two Air Defense squadrons, the USAF Tactical fighter Weapons Center at Nellis Air Force Base in Nevada, the USAF Tactical Air Warfare Center at Eglin Air Force Base in Florida and the USAF Air Defense Weapons Center, also in Florida at Tyndall Air Force Base. The 57th Fighter Interceptor Squadron from the Air Forces Iceland at

Above: Tactical Air Command Headquarters building at Langley Air Force Base. *(US Air Force)*

Keflavik, Iceland, is also an extraordinary unit of the TAC. The US has maintained a base on Iceland since 1951 when the two countries signed a defense agreement. The McDonnell Douglas F-15C Eagles stationed here fulfill the task of defending Iceland and its Military Air Defence Identification Zone (MADIZ), together with the defense of NATO's vital Atlantic sea lanes.

William Tell in Florida

Since the middle of the 1970s, tactical training, the TAC's second major task, has put more and more emphasis on fighter pilot proficiency in air superiority and air defense. So once every two years the TAC organizes an air defense exercise at the USAF Air Defense Weapons Center at Tyndall Air Force Base, Florida, in which NORAD squadrons, and very often PACAF and USAFE squadrons, take part. During the exercise, code-named 'William Tell', aircraft such as low-flying SAC B-52 bombers simulate hostile attacks that must be intercepted and new air defense tactics are put to the practical test often with unmanned aircraft as the targets. These drones are old jet fighters fitted with a radio receiver and a guidance computer. They are flown to the exercise area over the Gulf of Mexico by their 'pilots' — radio controllers on the ground. William Tell exercises use up a large number of drones, so many that stocks of types such as the PQM-102 Delta Dagger and the QF-100 Super Sabre are gradually being used up, and Convair F-106 Delta Darts and even McDonnell Douglas F-4 Phantoms are now being converted into unmanned target aircraft.

Hostile Russians over the desert

The experiences of the Vietnam War led the TAC to develop a number of realistic exercise programmes that it calls 'Flags'. The most well known and certainly the most realistic of these is Red Flag which is held several times a year at the large Nellis Air Force Base just north of the gambling city of Las Vegas in the Nevada desert. During the two-week exercise up to 250 aircraft fly a total of 3,500 missions. This extremely tough exercise is played under simulated war conditions and is aimed primarily at increasing the fighter pilots' chances of survival. In the Red Flag mock air battles top pilots fly the 'hostile' aircraft. The hostiles are very often Northrop F-5E Tiger II fighters which are similar in size and performance to the Russian MiG-21 Fishbed, the fighter much used by the Warsaw Pact air forces, although the F-16 Fighting Falcon is now used as well as it corresponds with the modern Russian MiG-29 Fulcrum in service with several Warsaw Pact air forces.

During the air battles, or dog fights, the aggressors make use of typical Soviet fighting tactics and their aircraft are generally painted in Russian or Warsaw Pact camouflage colours and designs. To make the event even more realistic, communication between the 'hostile' aircraft is in perfect Russian. Red Flag, in which NATO air forces may also participate, is not completely risk-free. The dog fights can end in collision and tragedy.

Above: General Dynamics F-16s from the 8th Tactical Fighter Wing at Kunsan Air Base in the Republic of Korea. The 'Wolf Pack' F-16s are seen here while refuelling from a Boeing KC-135A Stratotanker from the Strategic Air Command. *(General Dynamics)*

Top: The F-15C Eagles from the 57th Fighter Interceptor Squadron (Air Forces Iceland) are part of the Tactical Air Command.
(McDonnell Douglas)

Right: One single Boeing B-52 Stratofortress can carry up to 12 AGM-86 Air Launched Cruise Missiles (ALCMs). *(Boeing)*

The Strategic Air Command

The origins of the Strategic Air Command (SAC), possibly the most famous of the air commands, can be found in World War 2 when the 8th and 15th Air Forces in Europe and the 20th Air Force in the Pacific area began making strategic strikes on German and Japanese targets.

The conventional bombardments of the Boeing B-17 Flying Fortresses and Consolidated B-24 Liberators reduced cities to rubble. The atom bombs that the Boeing B-29 Superfortresses of the 509th Composite Group dropped on Hiroshima and Nagasaki virtually reduced these cities to a shadow, a devastating effect the equal of which was unknown in strategic warfare. At the end of World War 2 the US, as the only country with atomic weapons, had the monopoly on nuclear deterrence. In March 1946, seven months after the strikes on Hiroshima and Nagasaki, the SAC was made an independent air command and with this was given responsibility for the practical exploitation of the American nuclear deterrent. To enable it to do the job, in 1947 the SAC was allocated more than two thousand B-29s.

The Convair B-36 Peacemaker that came into service in 1948, gave the SAC intercontinental atomic strike capability. With its 13,000 kilometer flying range, the giant Peacemaker, of which the SAC had 385 up to 1958, could reach just about every corner of the globe. From just one of its bases, Eielson Air force Base near Fairbanks, Alaska, Peacemakers could, if necessary, strike anywhere within the Soviet Union, while B-36s at the Andersen Base on Guam covered the entire Pacific basin.

During the 1950s piston-engined bombers were gradually replaced by modern jet-powered bombers. For tactical nuclear attacks and reconnaissance the SAC acquired light jet bombers such as the Martin B-57 Canberra and the Douglas B-66 Destroyer. Later many hundreds of Boeing B-47 Stratojets were also taken into service as replacements for the B-29 bombers. Through the introduction of the LGM-25 Titan and LGM-80 Minuteman intercontinental nuclear missiles the strategic value of the Stratojet and later the large Boeing B-52 Stratofortress long-range bomber decreased more and more. Although the B-52G and B-52H can function as low-flying launching platforms for the Boeing AGM-86 Air Launched Cruise Missile (ALCM), the SAC's B-52s are gradually being converted for non-nuclear missions and it now looks as if, as far as the SAC is concerned, the days of the rapidly obsolescing B-52 are numbered.

The B-52s' successors are the Rockwell B-1B and the Northrop B-2. The B-2, which was built in the deepest possible secrecy, is of the 'flying wing' type and is popularly known as the 'Stealth Bomber'. According to experts, even the Russian's hyper-modern air defense can do nothing against the B-2. Due to its special shape and the application of modern materials such as carbons, the B-2's radar cross-section (RCS) is only a fraction of the B-52's. This means that radar systems can only detect it with the greatest difficulty. Or not at all. The 132 B-2s that Northrop will deliver — Congress permitting — to the United States Air Force from 1993 on will form the backbone of the SAC until well into the next century.

With its 110,000 personnel the SAC is one of the largest US Air Commands. From its Headquarters at Offutt Air Force Base near Omaha, Nebraska, around a thousand Minuteman and Peacekeeper intercontinental ballistic missiles and fifteen Wings with 350 strategic bombers are held at the ready 24 hours a day.

ORGANIZATION UNITED STATES AIR FORCE

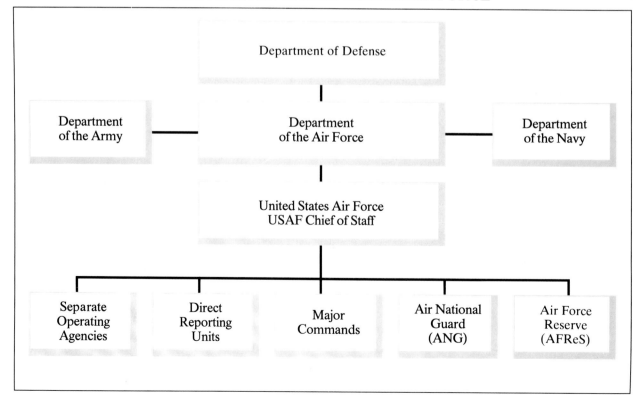

Above: In 1983 the Alaska Air Command switched over to McDonnell Douglas F-15 Eagles. The fighters of the 21st Tactical Fighter Wing are based at Elmendorf Air Force Base, but the forward operating locations (FOLs) Galena Airport, King Salmon Airport, Kotzebue Air Station and the Shemya Air Force Base on the Aleutian Islands are also used for operations. *(McDonnell Douglas)*

Right: The AFRes uses modern fighters such as this General Dynamics F-16A from the 466th Tactical Fighter Squadron at Hill Air Force Base, Utah. *(Ton van Schaik)*

Over the Himalayas and to Berlin

The history of the Military Airlift Command (MAC) began in May 1941 when the Air Corps Ferrying Command (ACFC) was set up to co-ordinate the Atlantic 'ferry flights' of the American combat aircraft destined for the British Royal Air Force. The ACFC, or Air Transport Command (ATC) as it was renamed a year later, was responsible for almost all air transport during World War 2. Although the ATC was capable of providing Atlantic cargo flights with its converted Consolidated B-24 Liberator bombers, most of the American material was shipped to England in the Atlantic convoys and the ATC did not play any significant role during the build-up of the American/Canadian invasion force in England.

In Indo-China, however, the ATC had a star part. Its Indo-China Division was responsible for supplying both the Chinese Chungking government and the American Air Force units operating from China. From its bases in India the ATC maintained an extensive air bridge that was nicknamed 'The Hump' because its route crossed the highest peaks in the Himalayas. Literally every item needed for the American war activities in China was flown in, even the fuel and bombs for the B-29 strikes on the Japanese mainland.

Extensive though The Hump was, it was overtaken in sheer size by Operation 'Vittles': the Berlin Airlift of 1948-49. During the fifteen months of Vittles, the Military Air Transport Service, the new Air Command that had replaced the ATC, made nearly 150,000 flights with Douglas C-47 Skytrain and Douglas C-54 Skymasters and transported 1.8 million tons of food and fuel, etc.

The cloak for cloak and dagger activities?

According to official figures, the MAC has at its command more than 1,000 transport aircraft, most of them Lockheeds. For short and medium range flights 300 C-130 Hercules aircraft in different versions are used and for long-range flights 270 C-141 Starlifters and 127 giant C-5 Galaxies. Over the past few years personnel figures have stabilized at around 92,000 although, if the transport units of the AFRes and ANG are mobilized, the MAC can count on an additional 400 aircraft and 60,000 personnel. Roughly speaking, the MAC's workshop is the whole world, a statement that is supported by the fact that the Command has more than 350 transport bases in over 24 countries. The MAC's world-wide operations are divided over the 21st and 22nd Air forces. The 21st Air Force is responsible for everywhere east of the US (Greenland, Iceland, Europe, Africa and the Middle East up to Iran and the Arabian peninsula) and south of the US (the Caribbean and South America). The 22nd Air Force is responsible for everywhere west of the US (Japan, South-East Asia, India, Pakistan and the Eastern areas of Saudi Arabia and Africa) plus Antarctica.

The 23rd Air Force is an extraordinary organization that was set up just a few years ago. This air force, an organizational unit of the MAC, spends most of its time on Special Operations, search and rescue and 'all actions that are necessary to support the national objectives' (quote from MAC Fact Sheet, March 1983).

This includes Unconventional Warfare (psychological and chemical warfare?) and Foreign Internal Defense (infiltration and espionage?). For these tasks the 23rd Air Force commands a goodly number of C-130 Hercules aircraft that may, once in a while, carry freight. The cargo makes a good cover for illegal activities — the cloak and dagger operations.

There are also Hercules that have been converted to AC-130H Gunships. These aircraft, also known as Spectres, have two 20 mm Vulcan cannons, one 40 mm Bofors gun and one 105 mm howitzer. Spectres were first used during the Vietnam War but since then have been used for clandestine operations, over El Salvador in 1982, for example. And what about the MC-130E Combat Talons stationed at Clark air base in the Philippines and Rhein Main air base near Frankfurt in the FRG? Their equipment includes the Fulton recovery system which enables them to pick up agents in hostile territory in full flight.

At the moment the 23rd Air Force is preparing for an extensive modernization. New aircraft will improve the Special Operations force's operational capabilities considerably. The new Lockheed MC-130H Combat Talon II will have even more electronic sensors than its predecessor, including infra-red apparatus for night operations and advanced terrain-following radar which will allow it to fly very low and therefore outside the reach of hostile radar. It is noteworthy that the new Combat Talon II will not be fitted with the Fulton recovery system. In the 1990s most infiltration tasks will be carried out by Bell/Boeing CV-22 tilt rotor aircraft; a combination of a helicopter and an aircraft with two tiltable motors that allow it to take off and land like a helicopter but fly like a normal plane. The CV-22 will be equipped with the advanced LANTIRN (Low Altitude Navigation and Targeting Infra-red system for Night) night navigation system.

New gunships are also on the way. These new Lockheed AC-130U Spectre will be fitted with GAU-12 25 mm rapid-firing cannons, a Bofors 40 mm gun and a 105 mm howitzer. It will also have the same APG-70 on-board radar as the McDonnell Douglas F-15E Strike Eagle which will give it all-weather capability.

Top cover for America

Alaska, separated from the Soviet Union only by the width of the Bering Strait — a distance of less than one hundred kilometers is America's most strategically located state. And in the Soviet Union there is a fleet of long range bombers comprising around 400 Bear, Bison, Backfire and the hyper-modern Blackjack aircraft plus approximately 300 Badger and Blinder medium-range bombers the Soviet Union holds in reserve.

According to the NORAD Headquarters at Peterson Air Force Base, Colorado springs, Colorado, NORAD has installed radar systems in Alaska that can penetrate deep into the Soviet Union, picking up aircraft movements as far away as the Verkhoyansky Mountains and over the Kamchatka Peninsula. By using a technique whereby the transmitted radar signals reflect off the outermost air layers of the atmosphere these radar systems can 'see' over the horizon and bridge distances of up to 5,000 kilometers. NORAD has also

The NORAD command post is located deep in the Cheyenne mountain complex. Here the information from the DEW-radars is compiled and processed. All data, such as interceptions of Soviet aircraft, is presented on large VDUs, left in the picture.
(Peterson Air Force Base)

built such a radar station near the Shemya air base on the westernmost Aleutian island in the Bering Sea. A large number of the USAF's Alaskan-mainland radar stations also form part of the Distant Early Warning (DEW) Line — the NORAD radar-chain that spreads over a distance of nearly 6,000 kilometers from Point Lay in North-west Alaska to the east coast of Greenland.

Information from these radar stations is transmitted to the Elmendorf Air Force Base near Anchorage. Elmendorf, the Alaskan Air Command's most vital base, houses the AAC headquarters and the Alaskan NORAD Region (ANR) control center. In the ANR center the radar information in assessed and, if it is deemed necessary, the ANR Commander orders an interception sortie to identify approaching aircraft.

Under the motto 'Top Cover for America' the McDonnell Douglas F-15 Eagles of the 21st Tactical Fighter Wing (TFW) scramble or take off on interception sorties. The fighters are armed with radar-guided Sparrow air-to-air missiles than can hit targets up to 100 kilometers away with spine-chilling precision.

The 21st TFW's F-15s frequently operate from the Shemya and Eielson air bases near Fairbanks. The Eielson air base houses the 343rd Composite Wing — a combined unit that includes the 18th Tactical Fighter Squadron (TFS), equipped with A-10 Thunderbolt II aircraft. Because it is so remote, Eielson is a superb base for the SAC's Boeing RC-135 spy planes. In this region where winter temperatures of below minus 50° Centigrade are far from unusual, these professional peeping toms do not have to worry about a great deal of outside interest.

The Pacific Air Force

The Pacific Air Force (PACAF) is — geographically — the USAF's largest Air Command. From PACAF Headquarters at Hickam, AFB, Hawaii, flying operations throughout the Pacific region, including the Indian Ocean, are managed. This is an operations zone of around 170 million square kilometers; an area approximately eighteen times larger than the United States itself. Despite the size of its operational area, the PACAF commands just 36,500 men and around 350 aircraft (mainly fighters) spread over ten main bases including ones in the Republic of Korea, Japan and the Philippines. The PACAF also operates a great many support posts on smaller islands such as Midway, Wake and Guam. The PACAF fighters are divided over the 5th and 13th Air Forces. The 13th Air Force is headquartered at Clark Air Force Base, north of Manila, in the Philippines. Units operating from Clark include the 3rd Tactical Fighter Wing, equipped with F-4E Phantoms. The 5th Air Force, the largest organization within PACAF, is headquartered at Yokota Air Base, Japan. The 5th Air Force comprises two divisions; the 313th Air Division based at Kadena, Okinawa and the 314th Air Division based at Osan Air Force Base, Korea. As part of the modernization programme it has undergone during the past few years, the 313th Air Division of the 5th Air Force has acquired F-15 Eagles at Kadena Air Base and F-16 Fighting Falcons at Misawa Air Base, Japan. The 314th Air Division in Korea also has F-16s. These belong to the so-called Wolfpack Unit at Kunsan Air Base.

★　★　★

Air war in Vietnam

The PACAF played a vital role throughout the Vietnam War. Shortly after the start of the North Vietnamese Tet Offensive in the spring of 1968 when the war was at its peak, the PACAF commanded nearly 175,000 personnel and 1,882 aircraft. The PACAF had had combat aircraft stationed at Tan Son Nhut air base just north of Saigon since 1961/1962. These were McDonnell RF-101 Voodoo reconnaissance aircraft and Convair F-102 Delta Dagger interceptor/fighters. The reconnaissance aircraft were used over Laos and South Vietnam to photograph Communist troop movements. The Daggers were only stationed in South Vietnam as precaution: at the time there was no thought of actually fighting.

Attack on the USS Maddox

After the North Vietnamese torpedoed the USS *Maddox* in the Gulf of Tonkin on 2 August 1964, the conflict in which the American Air Force had so far only played a minor role took a drastic turn. And after the USS *Turner Joy* was attacked two days later while patrolling the North Vietnamese coast, the US Navy 7th Fleet launched LTV F-8 Crusader fighter bomber for retaliation strikes on North Vietnamese navy bases and storage depots. Tension, naturally, skyrocketed and as a precautionary measure the American Defense Secretary, Robert McNamara, ordered a squadron of Republic F-105 Thunderchief fighters from Yokota, Japan, to Korat Air Base, Thailand. At the same time Martin B-57 bombers and North American F-100 Super Sabres were stationed at the South Vietnamese Bien Hoa and Danang Air Bases. A North Vietnamese reply to this American show of force was then only a matter of time.

That reply was delivered on 31 October 1964 in the form of a night mortar attack on Bien Hoa by the Vietcong in the course of which five B-57s were lost and thirteen were damaged, several severely. This Vietcong retaliation put pressure on the Americans to take countermeasures and plans were drawn up,although action was not yet forthcoming.

Operation 'Rolling Thunder'

PACAF did react to the attacks carried out by Pathet Lao guerrillas in neighbouring Laos. In December 1964 F-100 Super Sabres took off from Da Nang air base in South Vietnam and Takhli air base in Thailand for strikes against Pathet Lao supply lines. These strikes, code-named 'Barrel Roll', were the first of the long, hopeless series of American air offensives that continued throughout the Vietnam conflict. Strikes were also targeted on the North Vietnamese Ho Chi Minh supply line that ran from North Vietnam, straight through the almost impenetrable jungles of Laos and Cambodia (now Kampuchea), to South Vietnam.

The conflict gradually escalated until both sides were embroiled in bitter offensives. In 1965, in an attempt to bring the Vietcong to a standstill, PACAF began a sustained air offensive aimed at military installations, supply lines, etc, code-named 'Rolling Thunder'.

The Vietcong's Tet offensive in 1968 was repulsed, but only at the cost of a great number of lives, both American and South Vietnamese. Back in the US opposition to this, according to many, hopeless war was growing rapidly. On 1 November 1968 President Johnson, partly in deference to public opinion, ordered Operation Rolling Thunder bombardments stopped. But the North Vietnamese did not stop. On the contrary, over the following four years assaults on Laos and South Vietnam by North Vietnamese army and air force units increased. And on 16 April 1972, President Nixon reversed this decision and gave the order for Operation 'Linebacker'; a campaign aimed at bringing Hanoi to the negotiation table.

It looked as if it would work. So in October, in anticipation of the talks that were to be held in Paris, Linebacker operations were stopped. North Vietnam, however, saw in this US moratorium nothing more than an opportunity for military recuperation. The US reaction was to bomb Hanoi and Haiphong. 200 mighty Boeing B-52 strategic bombers from the SAC's 8th Air Force at U Tapao air base in Thailand and Andersen air base on Guam carried out the bombing campaign code-named 'Linebacker II'. This devastating series of attacks, which continued without respite for eleven days, forced North Vietnam back to the negotiation table and finally, on 28 January 1973 a peace treaty was signed.

Rapid reinforcement

In times of crisis the USAF can count on a substantial reserve formed by the Air Force Reserve (AFRes) and the Air National Guard (ANG). Within the framework of the USAF's Total Force Strategy, that came into power in 1973, AFRes and ANG units held at the ready can mobilize very quickly and, together with units of the USAF, can operate as one Air Force (Total Force). Although the tasks of both reserve units are similar there are essential differences.

The AFRes as the air force's reserve is directly attached to the USAF while the ANG belongs to the national reserve. The ANG's units are spread across all fifty states and are under the command of the relevant State Governor. The 64,000 AFRes reservists, having completed their service in the USAF, sign on for a number of extra years and provide services on a full-time basis primarily to the Military Airlift Command. Together with their USAF colleagues they fly and maintain MAC front line transport aircraft, such as the giant Lockheed C-5 Galaxy and the Lockheed C-141 Starlifter. While the large transport aircraft on intercontinental flights are often flown by purely AFRes crews, many other missions are flown by combined USAF/AFRes crews.

According to the Total Force Order, in times of national emergency, intercontinental tension or war, the AFRes must immediately make combat-ready units and trained personnel available to the USAF. To fulfil this obligation the AFRes, at the beginning of 1990, has eleven Wings with a total of around 230 fighters including modern F-16s and A-10s. In the event of mobilization, these squadrons are immediately transferred to the Tactical Air Command. There are also fourteen AFRes transport squadrons with 140 Lockheed C-130 Hercules medium weight transport aircraft, three squadrons with Boeing KC-135 Stratotankers, three

Defense minister Robert McNamara sent Republic F-105 Thunderchiefs to Thailand in 1964. These F-105Ds from the 355th Tactical Fighter Wing based at Takhli Air Base took part in the Barrel Roll and Rolling Thunder campaign against the Vietcong. *(Republic)*

squadrons with McDonnell Douglas KC-10 Extenders and seven squadrons with a variety of aircraft equipped for weather research, search and rescue, etc. During periods of tension the transport squadrons are under command of the MAC while the KC-135 and KC-10 tankers are commanded by the SAC.

In the 1970s, the air combat forces of the Warsaw Pact were increased and now the combined air forces of the Warsaw Pact countries are estimated at 7,240 fighters. In times of crisis these forces can be reinforced within fourteen hours with the 750 (reserve) aircraft kept in the central Soviet Union for this purpose.

According to official NATO lists, NATO's combined air forces (including France) command over 3,625 combat aircraft. The US and Canada can, between them, field 1,900 extra aircraft. 'Rapid Reinforcement' is the strategy developed for getting these aircraft to Europe as quickly as possible. The majority of these reinforcements are supplied by the ANG. To test their readiness, exercises during which ANG squadrons are sent to NATO bases in Europe for several weeks, often without any prior warning, are held every year under the code-name 'Coronet'.

Only at the weekend

The ANG comprises more than 160,000 militia-servicemen, all of whom are volunteers serving in their spare time. This has led to the ANG being mocked as the 'Weekend Air Force'. For a weekend air force the ANG is surprisingly large: 91 squadrons with a total of 1,460 aircraft (more than the air forces of Norway, Denmark, the Netherlands and Belgium together), several special squadrons for training, search and rescue, etc, ten squadrons with 170 interceptor fighters for the NORAD Command and an additional 65 tactical squadrons and thirteen tanker squadrons available for Rapid Reinforcement.

Right: The LTV A-7Ds from the Air National Guard will be modified to serve well into the nineties. Here four A-7Ds from the 121st Tactical Fighter Wing, Ohio Air National Guard, line up for a refuelling rendezvous with a Boeing KC-135. *(Ton van Schaik)*

Below: The Lockheed F-117 Stealth fighter made its public appearance in the spring of 1990. The aircraft was kept secret for almost ten years. *(DoD)*

Bottom: A formation of two McDonnell Douglas RF-4C photo-reconnaissance aircraft from the 165th Tactical Reconnaissance Squadron, Kentucky Air National Guard. With ten others, these RF-4Cs took part in the Coronet Bishop deployment (1983) to Ingolstadt air base, Germany. *(Archive Cees Steijger)*

Chapter 2
The European air wars

In 1917, when the first American troops were sent to the European theatre to fight alongside the Allies against the German Army, the war in Europe had already been raging for three years. The United States did not, in fact, want to take part in this war. Or rather it was not President Woodrow Wilson's intention and for a long time he succeeded in his aim of preserving the US's neutrality. But the tension could be cut with a knife because, despite this neutrality, the German submarines which were attacking merchant shipping in the Atlantic Ocean made absolutely no distinction between English, French or American vessels. The US's right as a neutral power to freedom of the seas was blatantly ignored by the Germans whose only response to furious American protest was that they would curtail the Kriegsmarine's activities in the international shipping lanes as much as possible.

If there was any curtailment it was hardly noticeable. The German U-boats continued making the oceans dangerous places to be. Public opinion in the US began to turn sharply against Germany and there was no longer any doubt that the US would declare war on Germany, it was only a question of when. Pressure from his electors eventually forced President Wilson away from his stance of passive observer and he asked the American Congress to declare war on Germany. The answer was not long in coming. The US declared war on Germany on 6 April 1917 and became involved in World War 1.

Not much of an air force

General John J. Pershing was given command of the American Expeditionary Forces, formed very quickly and sent to France. Pershing, an old army hand who had earned his spurs during the American-Spanish war of 1889, appointed Brigadier-General Mason M. Patrick Chief of Staff of the Air Service in France. His command did not actually amount to much, as ten years after its formation the entire American air force comprised just seven squadrons with a total of 250 aircraft, most of which were completely outdated and totally unsuitable for hostilities such as those taking place in France.

Compared to the French Aéronautique Militaire and the British Royal Flying Corps, which in 1917 could field about 3,000 aircraft each, the American air force

was nothing. Both France and Britain put great pressure on the US, urging them to participate in the fight with a more extensive Air Service. In response, the US developed ambitious plans for the production of at least 22,265 aircraft, with spare parts, and 44,000 aircraft engines for a total estimated cost of $640 million. In addition, the American air force would grow from seven squadrons to no fewer than 426 combat squadrons.

According to the plans, 263 squadrons would be stationed in France by June 1918. The first task force to arrive in Europe was the 1st Aero Group. The troops and material were embarked in New York harbour on 17 August 1917 and arrived in Le Havre on 3 September. The Americans were sent to the relatively tranquil Toul-Rosières where French Spad XIII biplanes had been brought to a state of readiness for them and from where, after several months of intensive training, they made their first operational flights on 3 April 1918.

The American Lafayette volunteers

The pilots of the 1st Aero Group were not, however, the first Americans to fly missions against the German flyers. This honour went to the American volunteers who had enlisted with the French Aéronautique Militaire much earlier in the war. These volunteers were a mixed bunch. but whether they were 'Go-East' pioneers from the US or young American men from the French Foreign Legion, these flying enthusiasts had one thing in common: they were without exception in search of fame and glory and hoped to find them in France.

The first American volunteers arrived in France around the end of 1914. Although it was certainly not usual for the French military to accept foreigners, several of them succeeded in being accepted into the Aéronautique Militaire and posted to various units. This did not suit the American contingent who preferred to stay together and they very quickly let it be known that they wanted to form a unit made up exclusively of their compatriots. After several initial problems were overcome the French government voted the unit into being in April 1916. The way was open for the new American squadron to be established. A squadron that was very quickly dubbed the Escadrille Americaine.

A Spad (foreground) and a Nieuport fighter aircraft from the
Escadrille Lafayette, on an airfield somewhere near the Somme.
(Service Historique de l'Armée de l'Air)

The escadrille was assembled at the French Luxeuil airfield west of Mulhouse and 175 kilometres from the front at Verdun. At Luxeuil French Nieuport fighters were put at the disposal of the Americans. Training in these French biplanes took just a few weeks and very soon the escadrille was carrying out patrol flights around Mulhouse.

The formation of the Escadrille Americaine N124 (N for Nieuport) drew immediate and fierce protest from the German camp. The Germans took their strong objections to the active participation of the neutral United States in the war straight to the top. The government in Washington put a high value on America's neutrality and the preservation of the highly favoured Monroe Doctrine (no meddling in the affairs of other countries). There was no question of official American participation in the war and the US definitely did not want to be drawn into the European conflict, especially not through such an inane business as the squadron name of a group of American volunteer pilots. So as not to compromise themselves, the American High Command urgently requested a change of name for the Escadrille Americaine. The message was understood in Paris and the search for a solution began at once. The first name suggested was Escadrille des Voluntaires: hardly original and not accepted. Eventually the name Escadrille Lafayette, in honour of the famous general who fought on Washington's side in the American Civil War, was chosen.

★   ★   ★

Indians over the Somme

The Escadrille Lafayette was a unit of the French Aéronautique Militaire and was, logically, equipped with Nieuport fighter aircraft. Later the escadrille also received the somewhat superior Spad, the biplane fighter with which at least 81 other French escadrilles were equipped. Later the American Expeditionary Force also commanded sixteen squadrons equipped with this aircraft. The Spad's two nose-mounted machine-guns, like those of the Fokker E.III monoplane, were fitted with interrupters which enabled the salvoes to go past the wooden propeller blades rather than into them.

Initially the Nieuports and Spads of the Escadrille Lafayette were used for patrol flights, until the summer of 1916 only in the Mulhouse area, but then also over the front around Verdun. At the end of 1916, during the French/British offensive in the Somme region, the escadrille was transferred to the Cachy airfield from where they flew over the bloody Somme battlefield. Very probably it was at Cachy that the aircraft were first decorated with an emblem: first a representation of a Seminole Indian and later a Sioux Indian. Until the end of the war the Lafayette Indians flew many sorties over the front. Flying from the Ravenal airfield near St. Just-en-Chassée they provided air support for the 1917 New Year's offensive, and several months later they were actively involved in the fighting round Ieper in Belgium from St. Pol-sur-mer.

An unknown American volunteer in France searching for glory.
(US Air Force)

As 1917 drew to a close the escadrille moved once again to a new airfield North of Châlons-sur-Marne from where it went into action for the last time prior to February 1918 when it was disbanded from within the Aéronautique Militaire and incorporated into the American Expeditionary Forces as the 103rd Pursuit Squadron. Between 1916 and 1918 the Lafayette volunteers carried out many missions against the German Fliegertruppen, achieving for the escadrille an impressive score of 38 air victories. Even now there are still Lafayette Indians in the air over France because, in memory of the American volunteers, the Dassault-Breguet Mirage 2000N bombers of the 4th Wing of l'Armee de l'Air at the Luxeuil AB (where the Escadrille Lafayette began) still carry the Sioux emblem.

★　　★　　★

Problems for General Patrick

General Patrick's problems began almost as soon as the first unit of the Air Service arrived in Le Havre in September 1917. Due to the speed of the build-up there was a great shortage of material and, far more worrying, there were too few pilots. That was, of course, a direct result of the American Army Command's aviation policy — or rather, lack of it. In the US, military aviation received little government support although, to be honest, in the US it was not really necessary. It was a different story in Europe where international tensions resulted in military armament, particularly in France, Germany and England, taking on a grand shape and where very early on the military command saw the advantages of incorporating aircraft into their combat forces.

It is true that initially balloons were used by the army, primarily as artillery observation platforms, but aircraft were very soon introduced. More manoeuvrable, more versatile and far more mobile than balloons, aircraft could be used close to the front for observation, reconnaissance and later even for bombardment of enemy installations. After very little hesitation the French Aéronautique Militaire, the British Royal Flying Corps and the German Fliegertruppen equipped themselves with hundreds of aircraft. By comparison, in the summer of 1914, the Aeronautical Division of the American Army commanded less than twenty combat aircraft and about thirty experienced pilots.

Three years later, when it was very clear that they could not catch up overnight, the American High Command could do no other than appeal to the French and British war industries. Pending supply from the US, large numbers of combat aircraft were bought from France (Spads and Nieuports) and England (Sopwith Camels). So, despite the shortage of American materials, the Air Service units in France were soon equipped, albeit with a mixed collection of aircraft, and could support the French troops during Germany's New Year Somme and Marne offensive.

DES AVIATEURS AMERICAINS OFFRENT LEURS SERVICES A LA FRANCE

Il y a quelques jours, un groupe d'une dizaine de jeunes aviateurs américains ayant fait partie pendant la Grande guerre de l'escadrille Lafayette faisaient connaître au ministre de la Guerre qu'ils seraient désireux de combattre au Maroc pour la cause de la France.

Ils ont été reçus hier par le général Jacquemont, chef du cabinet militaire de M. Painlevé, qui, après les avoir chaleureusement remerciés de leur proposition, les a informés que le ministre de la Guerre accueillait avec reconnaissance leur offre généreuse. La seule formalité à remplir consistera pour eux à se mettre à la disposition du sultan du Maroc. La loi qui permettait, pendant la guerre, de procéder à l'incorporation des étrangers dans les régiments français est devenue caduque.

Les aviateurs yankees, qui ont accepté cette façon de procéder, seront très prochainement incorporés dans l'armée chérifienne.

Article from Le Monde in 1916 (precise date of publication is not known). Several American pilots volunteered for 'La Cause de le France' and left France to fight for the Sultan of Morocco.

American offensive

In the summer of 1918 the stream of reinforcements from the US finally began to really flow. Enough pilots and mechanics arrived in France for around 25 squadrons to be formed and many hundreds of thousands of American Expeditionary force troops prepared themselves for a massive offensive against the battle-weary German armies which were holding the front at St. Mihiel and Verdun. A large-scale combined American/French assault on the German lines in the Argonne forests between Clermont and Vouziers were also in preparation. Success in this combined autumn offensive would, according to many, bring General Erich Ludendorff's army into such difficulties that it would soon be forced to surrender.

On 12 September 1918 the Americans, under the command of General Pershing, attacked at Verdun and St. Mihiel. The entrenched German army held out against the onslaught of the strong, young, allied troops for just four days before surrendering.

This rapid victory over the German troops was an important motivating factor for the conflict that lay ahead; the combined American/ French Argonne offensive was due to start in just ten days time. In the battle for the Argonne, which historians often consider as decisive for the result of the war, the Germans, faced by large numbers of ground troops plus hundreds of aircraft that took to the skies almost daily in support, quickly lost ground. This powerful display of air support had only been made possible by reorganizing the American/French Army Air Forces. This reorganization, which boiled down to an organizational amalgamation of both air forces, was carried out by American General Mitchell who, as the new Commander in Chief of the Air Service* in France, took command of the American First Army's air operations.

In contrast to General Pershing, Mitchell did not advocate using aircraft solely to support ground troops.

He wanted to use them offensively to bombard targets of military or strategic importance and he set great store by air defense, a role for which the aircraft was ideally suited as was to be proven during the war. Mitchell commanded around fifty squadrons during the Argonne offensive, half of which were French, plus an air division of l'Armée de l'Air that comprised forty squadrons. He could also count on co-operation and support from the British Flying Corps. Although the exact number of aircraft Mitchell commanded has never been released, it is estimated at around 1,500. Enough, in any event, to help bring the German army to its knees.

Once Germany had surrendered and the cease-fire had been signed on 11 November 1918 in Compiegne, just north of Paris, the balance sheet could be tallied. The strength of the US Army Air Service in France was, at that time, approximately 740 combat aircraft (mainly French Spad biplanes), dispersed among 45 Fighter Squadrons. Of the eighty American pilots in service in France at that moment, 71 were Aces — pilots with more than five victories to their credit. Between them the American pilots had destroyed 781 aircraft and 73 balloons. The Americans' own losses in the first European air war were 289 aircraft and 48 balloons.

Top Ace Rickenbacker

Among the squadrons supporting the Argonne offensive was the famous American 94th Aero Squadron which in the last months of the war was commanded by Captain Eddie Rickenbacker. This top pilot already had eight victories to his credit — including four German Fokker D.VII biplane fighters — when on 25 September 1918 he became Commander of the 94th. During the last American offensive Rickenbacker in his Spad biplane notched up another eighteen victories. At the end of the war Rickenbacker's 26 victories ensured him the title of America's top Ace.

★　★　★

Mitchell court-martialled

As soon as the war was over demobilization of the Air Service began. The number of personnel was reduced from 200,000 to less than 10,000 and the many thousands of combat aircraft waiting in American harbours for shipment to Europe now waited for the scrapper's hammer instead. The Air Service's aircraft were reduced to just under 2,800, most of which, it should be mentioned, remained in storage where they soon became obsolescent. Just how little notice was taken of the Air Service can be judged from the fact that three years later the number of aircraft in active service was drastically reduced until only around 740 were left.

Under America's new military code, which came into force in 1920, the Air Service remained an integral unit of the American Army. This was in sharp contrast to the attention that focussed on the development of the US Navy which had, in the meantime, been given responsibility for protection of the US against invasion.

* The Air Service had, by then, ceased to be a unit of the Signal Corps. On 24 May 1918 it was, as US Army Air Service, promoted to an independent army unit of the same importance as the Signal Corps.

Many people disagreed with this situation but the man who decided to come out and fight it was Brigadier General Mitchell. Having commanded strategic air strikes in World War 1 which greatly contributed towards the allies' success, he promoted a separate air force independent of the land forces.

Mitchell was also determined to show that the Air Service was in far better position than the US Navy when it came to protecting the US from invasion and he was not adverse to using publicity stunts to put power behind his argument. On 13 July 1921 Mitchell had shown the Navy Staff how ships could be sunk by air strikes. A short while later he decided to show everyone else. First he had three ex-German Kriegs-marine battleships — including the reputedly unsinkable *Ostriesland* — sunk in Maryland's Chesapeake Bay by a single air strike. Then he used 28 Martin bombers to destroy an old German frigate. Two years later he organized a similar stunt, this time sinking two old US Navy battleships with a well judged air strike off the coast of North Carolina at Cape Hatteras.

Although Mitchell had once again demonstrated the possibilities of precision bombing, his activities and his criticism of the Army high command was hardly appreciated and certainly not supported. On the contrary. Mitchell went completely out of favour when he began denouncing the Military Command's policies. And shortly after a sad accident involving a large US Navy airship in September 1925, he went so far as to call the leaders of the Department of Defense's War and Navy Departments incompetent and their actions criminal. The military command highly resented these accusations and, as was only to be expected, Mitchell was soon court martialled for insubordination. Some time later he was removed from active service and with that, both Mitchell and his ideas on strategy were finished. As often happens, Mitchell's belief in the strategic role of aircraft was eventually vindicated, but not until the second half of the 1930s when German and Japanese war threats caused international tension to rise did the American army chiefs finally understand the necessity for a separate, strategic air force.

Roosevelt stays out of the fight

Franklin D. Roosevelt, the American President, had decided to keep the US out of all large-scale conflicts. He could really do little else because in 1937 the US was far from being prepared for a grand war. Military spending was at an absolute minimum: President Roosevelt was fighting the depression of the 1930s and needed a lot of money to finance his 'New Deal' reconstruction programme; the programme that was to turn the economy around. So in the 1936 budget year, spending for the US Army Air Corps, as the Air Service was now called, amounted to just $45 million. And although this was 65 per cent more than in the previous year, it was still completely inadequate to allow Brigadier General Frank M. Andrews to carry out his plans to expand the Air Corps — then sixth in world ranking — and equip it with up-to-date Boeing B-17 long-range bombers.

Roosevelt detested fascism, and with it the Axis countries, but he held on to the principle of non-involvement as laid down in the Neutrality Act of 1937.

The Sioux emblem on the portside of a Spad in 1917.
(Service Historique de l'Armée de l'Air)

Eddie Rickenbacker was the undisputed American top-ace in World War 1. He was commander of the famous 94th Aero Squadron named the 'Hat-in-the-ring' Squadron after its typical squadron emblem. *(US Air Force)*

Brigadier General William Mitchell became the new commander of the US Army Air Service in France. He wanted an airpower to carry out strategic bombing. *(US Air Force)*

When Germany invaded Poland on 1 September 1939 and war broke out, Roosevelt's proclamation of US neutrality was not wholehearted. It was not that Roosevelt could not read the signs of the times. On the contrary, in fact. Back in 1938 he had already warned the Americans of the Nazi threat and declared that America was no longer a 'distant continent'. A year later he would even say that the American border lay on the Rhine! Roosevelt foresaw that the fighting in Europe would escalate into a world-wide conflict and acknowledged that the US would become involved. His policy was, therefore, to provide the maximum of support to the enemies of fascism without actually voluntarily taking part in the war. From that moment he began to prepare America for the time it would be forced into a war.

In January 1939, Roosevelt, defending a plan before the Congress for extra defense spending, called the existing air force totally inadequate and stressed the need for immediate strengthening of the air fleet. Congress reacted promptly and of an extra $525 million that was due to be spent on the army and the navy, $300 million was made available for the acquisition of no fewer than 6,000 aircraft. Air Force General Andrews' plans were quickly taken out of the cupboard and in September 1939 while the German Luftwaffe was carrying out massive air strikes on Poland as part of the Blitzkrieg, the Air Corps was trying out its 38 brand new Boeing B-17 bombers. Still not many, but a start.

Cash and carry

The American Neutrality Act did not help Britain at all. The law forbade the export of the arms and ammunition that Britain, having declared war on Germany after the Nazi invasion of Poland, desperately needed. Luckily, in July 1939 Roosevelt had suggested that the arms embargo should be lifted. The amendment approved by the House of Representatives four months later, in November, included the so-called 'cash and carry' clause which allowed munitions to be supplied to Britain and France.

From then on, Presidential approval could supply arms and ammunition to countries that asked for them, on condition that the countries concerned came and fetched the arms with cash in their hands. So, as long as they paid for them at once, Britain and France could get all the arms and ammunition they wanted. On the surface a good agreement, but only as long as the money was available and in Britain, which had mobilized at high speed, money was in short supply. Towards the end of 1940, Britain's Prime Minister Winston Churchill told Roosevelt that Britain's cash flow problem would soon put a stop to cash and carry. President Roosevelt's reaction to this plea for help was his now famous 'garden hose address' delivered during a press conference: 'Imagine that fire breaks out at my neighbour's and I have a garden hose and I live 100 meters from him. If he can use my hose, on his own tap, then I am helping him put out the fire. What do I do in such a case? I obviously don't begin by saying, neighbour my garden hose cost fifteen dollars and you must pay me this first. No. What really happens? I don't want fifteen dollars, all I want is my hose back once the fire is put out.'

In this popular manner, President Roosevelt pleaded for the introduction of the famous Lend-Lease Act. This Act, passed by the House of Representatives in March 1941, empowered the President to allow war materials to be manufactured and once manufactured to be sold, lent or leased to any country the defense of which, in the judgement of the President, was of vital importance to the US.

Two weeks after the new law came into force, the first $7 billion was appropriated. Britain, the main large-scale beneficiary of the new Lend-Lease Act, received enormous quantities of munitions and thousands of weapons and vehicles via the Atlantic supply lines as well as many hundreds of aircraft, including Douglas C-47 Dakotas and Boeing B-17C Flying Fortresses, that were flown over for the Royal Air Force Transport and Bomber Commands.

Once the Soviet Union became involved in the War through Germany's surprise attack 'Barbarossa', it too made use of the Lend-Lease Act. Between the beginning of 1942 and the end of 1943, the US supplied the Red Air Force with at least five thousand Bell P-39 Airacobra combat aircraft; more than the Americans themselves would ever use. In its fight against Nazi Germany, the Soviet Union was, to a large extent, dependent on Lend-Lease materials. Its indignation was, therefore, great when in May 1945 American war aid was abruptly stopped. A simple action but one that was to have many consequences for the future.

Target: Germany

With vast amounts of war materials going to Britain and the Soviet Union, the North Atlantic shipping lanes, which ran southwards past Greenland and Iceland, became extremely busy. The German reaction which this open military support from still neutral America was bound to evoke, put the US in a difficult predicament.

The German Navy's U-boat strength in the seas around the supply routes was high and posed a dangerous threat to American merchant shipping. The situation worsened when the US took over the defense of Greenland and Iceland and set up local military bases. German submarine attacks were now to be expected. The first serious incident occurred on 4 September 1941 when the American destroyer USS *Greer* barely managed to escape from an attack by a German U-boat (*U-652*).

A week later Roosevelt authorised the fleet and the air force to attack on sight any Axis ship in 'US-interested' waters. His orders were carried out promptly and systematically. In this situation the US could hardly continue to consider itself a neutral power. Two months later the Neutrality Act was once again amended. American merchant ships were armed and authorized to sail through the war zones. It was clear that the US was gradually steeling itself for the decisive German blow that would draw it irrevocably into the conflict.

On 7 December 1941, the blow fell but on the other side of the world in a place where the Americans least expected it: Pearl Harbour, the largest American naval base in the Pacific Ocean. At 07:50 on Sunday, 7 December, the first Japanese bomb fell on the base.

The light German cruiser 'Frankfurt' was attacked on July 18, 1921. For more than five hours the Frankfurt was pummelled by the Navy and the Marine Corps 100- to 300-pound bombs, without serious damage to the cruiser. After an attack by six heavy Martin bombers, unloading their 600-pounders on the Frankfurt, the ship went down in just 35 minutes. *(US Air Force)*

Two hours later the attack launched from carriers had succeeded in putting the entire US Pacific Fleet's battleship force out of action. The next day a shaken America declared war on Japan. On 11 December Hitler declared war on America. The Axis satellites — Italy, Rumania, Hungary and Bulgaria — followed with declarations of war on 12 and 13 December. America was now firmly enmeshed in World War 2.

Churchill and Roosevelt had already met several times in secret to discuss the joint conduct of the war in the event of the US becoming involved in the conflict. They met again in January 1942, this time openly. During this series of summit meetings — code-named 'Arcadia', the Greek name for the land of peace and plenty — it was agreed that the British/American offensive needed to be directed against the Axis powers of Germany and Italy in the European Theatre of war and then, when the situation in Europe allowed, the attack against Japan would begin. America, Britain and her dominions could assemble the allied invasion force needed to open a second front in Europe. Germany had invaded the Soviet Union in June 1941 but 'Operation Barbarossa' had ground to a halt by December that year. Most importantly, a start could be made on building up a strategic air force in Britain and later North Africa and Italy, that could bomb and ultimately cripple the Axis war industry.

The 56th Fighter Group flew with the Republic P-47 Thunderbolt fighter.
This P-47D with code 'HV-P' was preserved after the war and
photographed in the seventies at Wright Patterson Air Force Base.
(Archive Cees Steijger)

Below: Boeing B-17 Flying Fortresses of the 8th Air Force depart from an
air base in England for a bombing mission over occupied Europe.
(US Air Force)

Strategic Bombing

In June 1941 President Roosevelt had approved the plan for the formation of a new, autonomous army division; the Army Air Forces (AAF) (although the Air Corps and Air Force Combat Command remained in being until 9 March 1942) and Major General Henry H. 'Hap' Arnold was given overall command. Arnold was a known supporter of Mitchell's ideas about strategic bombing and his open support of Mitchell had led to him being sideways promoted for several years by the Chiefs of Staff. In July 1941 the President asked the Secretaries of War and of the Navy to produce estimates for bringing their forces to an effective war footing. Arnold seized the opportunity to gain permission for the AAC's Air War Plans Division (AWPD) to prepare their own report, forcing the War Plans Division to concentrate solely on the needs of its land forces.

Arnold's staff officers at AWPD, headed by Colonel Harold L. George, formulated a policy (AWPD/1) of relentless air attacks against Germany, strategic defense in the Pacific Theatre and air operations in the defense of the Western Hemisphere. If Japan entered the war, it too would be subjected to aerial bombardment after Germany had surrendered.

The far thinking authors of AWPD/1, which also included Lt Colonel Kenneth Walker, Major Haywood Hansell and Major Laurence S. Kutler, listed 154 targets for its strategic bombing concept. First priority was given to Germany's electric power grid, followed in importance by its transportation system of rail, road and canals, then its oil and petroleum industry. It was argued that strategic bombing of these targets, together with the neutralization of the Luftwaffe, submarine and naval facilities might render a land campaign unnecessary.

The Air Corps received its first Boeing B-17s in 1939. The picture shows the YB-17 prototype of the legendary 'Flying Fortress' of which nearly 13,000 would be built in the period 1938-1945.
(US Air Force)

AWPD/1 calculated that 3,026 twin and four-engined bombers and 1,300 fighters based in Great Britain could achieve these objectives (together with a further 1,596 fighters and bombers in Egypt) using precision bombing as its weapon. AWPD/1 concluded that the AAF could mount a campaign in less than a year; half the time the Army needed to prepare for war in Europe.

General George Marshall, the Army Chief of Staff, reacted favourably to the plan and sent it straight to the Secretary of War, Henry Stimson, without first submitting it to the Army-Navy Joint Board. Stimpson rubber stamped AWPD/1 and a strategic bomber offensive against Germany became accepted as both AAF and US Government policy. Its weapon: precision bombing.

Bombing operations at the Tactical School, Bombardment Section, at Maxwell Field, Alabama, had largely adopted a strategic bombing doctrine, mainly through the instigation of its Chief, Captain Harold L. George, since 1931. Bomber aircraft development during the late 1930s also took the new strategy into account.

The Boeing Company had responded to an invitation in August 1934 by the US Army to take part in a competition for a new multi-engine (generally used to indicate two engines) bomber which could carry a bomb load of 2,000 lb for between 1,020-2,200 miles, at a speed of 200-250 mph. Boeing were already working on a four-engined design called the Model 299. Rushed to completion in only a year, the Model 299 flew for the first time on 28 July 1935. The Army later placed a service test order for 13 flight articles and a static test model under the designation YB-17.

The first Y1B-17s went into service during January-August 1937 with the 2nd Bombardment Group. Meanwhile, the US Army ordered the static test aircraft completed as a high-altitude bomber with turbo-supercharged engines. This was delivered as the Y1B-17A and resulted in a production order for thirty-eight B-17Bs. These were delivered to the 2nd and 7th Bomb Groups during October 1939-March 1940.

Meanwhile, early in 1939 the US Army Air Corps had drawn up a requirement for a new heavy bomber with a greatly improved range, some 3,000 miles, a top speed in excess of 300 mph and a ceiling of 35,000 feet. The Consolidated Company of San Diego, California submitted the LB-30, which was a landplane version of their Model 29 flying boat (PB2-Y). The Army Air Corps showed interest and it led to the XB-24, which incorporated a high aspect ratio wing and the twin-finned empennage used on the company's Model 31 flying boat (P4Y-1).

The XB-24 prototype flew for the first time on 29 December 1939. Seven YB-24s proved successful during service trials and an order was placed for thirty-six of the initial B-24 production version. Six YB-24s and twenty B-24As were diverted to the RAF and after the fall of France in June 1940, Britain took over the French contract for 139 LB-30s. Both the B-17 and the B-24 were greatly improved as a result of RAF experience gained in Europe in other combat types.

In 1940 the 2nd and 7th Groups equipped with Boeing B-17B high altitude bombers practised precision bombing using the top secret Norden bomb sight, developed by the US Navy, until experienced bombardiers could place their practice bombs within fifteen meters of the target from as high as 20,000 feet; a feat which led to claims that bombs could be placed in a pickle barrel from such heights. On the bomb run the bombardier took over flying the aircraft from the pilot

Even from high altitudes the Boeing B-17 could hit targets with great accuracy. *(US Air Force)*

by using the Automatic Flight Control Equipment (AFCE) which gave him lateral control of the aircraft through the Norden bombsight's connection to the auto-pilot.

Precision bombing called for attacks in daylight but the ideal conditions prevailing on the ranges at Muroc Dry Lake in the California Mojave Desert were not to be found in Europe where first the Luftwaffe and then RAF Bomber Command, had discovered that day bombing was too costly. During the first few months of the war unescorted RAF bombers on daylight raids fell easy victim to the Luftwaffe's Messerschmitt 109s and 110s and forced the British heavies to operate only at night.

John Pimlott, Professor of War Studies at Sandhurst, the British Army military academy, states in his book *Air Warfare* that when the RAF switched over to night raids, the term 'precision bombing' no longer applied. Although electronic aids were already being used, often RAF crews could not find and bomb their targets accurately in bad weather.

In 1942 Air Chief Marshal (later Sir Arthur) Harris, newly appointed head of RAF Bomber Command, instructed his crews to adopt area bombing methods using incendiaries to destroy German cities and break civilian morale. Lübeck and Rostock were razed to the ground and then on the night of 30/31 May 1,046 bombers, in the first of three RAF 'Thousand bomber' raids on German cities, wiped out two and a half square kilometers of Cologne. The fact that these raids severely reduced the Germans' ability to produce war materials by wiping out the work force was not lost on many senior officers in the US Air Forces. Later, they would also resort to fire bombing raids on German, and Japanese, cities, but with even more deadly effect.

Curtiss P-40 Warhawks like these were stationed at Reykjavik Air Base, Iceland, in September 1941. They belonged to the 33rd Pursuit Squadron and were used for the defense of the Atlantic sea lanes.
(US Air Force)

For the time being though, American strategists were convinced that enemy targets could be destroyed by daylight precision bombing. They believed that the heavily armed B-17 and B-24 fleets could fight their way to their targets without incurring prohibitive losses.

Home Sweet Home — England

Far-reaching decisions had been made in the event that America should become involved in the conflict with Germany. Between 27 January and 27 March 1941 agreements between the United States and Great Britain were made for the provision of naval, ground and air support for the campaign against Germany. As a result, a special US Army Observer Group, headed by Major General James E Chaney, was activated in London on 19 May 1941. One of Chaney's first tasks was to reconnoitre areas regarded as potential sites for US Army Air Force (USAAF) installations.

On 2 January 1942 the order activating the Eighth Air Force was signed by Major General Henry Arnold, the Commanding General, Army Air Forces and the headquarters was formed at Savannah, Georgia, on 28 January. The War Department in Washington announced that US ground forces were to be sent to Northern Ireland. On 8 January the activation of US Forces in the British Isles (USAFBI) was announced. Thirdly, a bomber command was to be established in England. Arnold instructed Brigadier-General Ira C. Eaker, who had spent a month in England in 1941 observing the RAF at close quarters, to assist in the formation of a headquarters for the American air forces in Great Britain. Eaker took up his duties as Commanding General of VIII Bomber Command in England in February 1942. Eaker's headquarters was

established at RAF Bomber Command Headquarters at High Wycombe where, on 22 February, VIII Bomber Command was formally activated.

While Eaker and his small team of relatively inexperienced officers decided about prospective air bases in eastern England, in America, B-17 and B-24 heavy bombardment groups were activated for deployment to Britain. Four B-17E/F groups: the 92nd, 97th, 301st, 303rd and two B-24D Liberator groups, the 44th and 93rd, formed the nucleus of the Eighth's heavy bombardment force in England.

First to arrive in the United Kingdom was the ground echelon of the 97th Bomb Group, which disembarked on 9 June and en-trained for their Polebrook base in Northamptonshire where earlier, RAF Fortress Is had taken off on raids over Germany. The 1st Fighter Group, equipped with the P-38 Lightning twin-tailed fighter, also arrived in England in June.

On 4 July, Independence Day, six American crews from the 15th Bombardment Group (Light) together with six RAF crews were despatched from RAF Swanton Morley, Norfolk, on a daylight sweep against four German airfields in Holland. It was the first time American airmen had flown in American-built bombers against a German target but although it was important historically, the raid was not an unqualified success. Two of the aircraft manned by Americans were shot down by what the RAF flight leader described as 'the worst flak barrage in my experience'.

In August 1942 the 92nd and 301st Bomb Groups arrived to join Eaker's rapidly increasing air force. The 92nd was the first heavy bombardment group to successfully make a non-stop flight from Newfoundland to Scotland. The 14th Fighter Group also arrived in England during June. (Despite flying over 340 Lightning sorties, the 1st and 14th Fighter Groups never encountered the enemy and both were transferred to support Operation Torch, the invasion of North-west Africa, in November 1942.)

General Ira C. Eaker was commander of B-17 'Yankee Doodle' during the first strategic attack of the 8th Air Force on 17 August 1942. Shortly after his arrival back on Polebrook Air Base General Eaker told his story to the press. *(US Air Force)*

It took time to get the new groups ready for combat and training was lacking in many areas. Colonel Frank A. Armstrong, one of Eaker's original HQ staff, was appointed CO of the 97th Bomb Group at Grafton Underwood at the end of July in place of Lt Colonel Cousland and he set about re-shaping the group. By mid-August he had 24 crews ready for combat. Meanwhile, as arguments went on behind the scenes about whether bombing in daylight was possible over heavily defended targets in Europe or even that the Fortresses' and Liberators' bomb carrying capacity and their armament would be enough, the first Fortresses strike of the war was scheduled for 17 August 1942.

General Carl 'Tooley' Spaatz, the American air commander in Europe, and members of his staff, attended the briefing at Grafton Underwood. At 15.00 hours six B-17Es took off from Polebrook and flew a diversionary raid on St. Omer. Briefing over at Underwood, Frank Armstrong boarded 'Butcher Shop' which was piloted by Major Paul Tibbets and led eleven B-17s to the marshalling yards at Rouen Sotteville in northwestern France. Spaatz had felt confident enough to allow Brigadier General Ira C. Eaker to fly on the mission. He joined the crew of 'Yankee Doodle', lead aircraft of the second flight of six. Over the Channel, the Fortresses were joined by their RAF escort of Spitfire Vs.

Visibility over the target was good and bombing was made from 23,000 feet. A few bombs hit a mile short of the target and one burst hit about a mile west in some woods but the majority landed in the assigned area. Several repair and maintenance workshops were badly damaged which temporarily put the German State Railway out of action.

First of the congratulatory messages to arrive came from Air Marshal Sir Arthur Harris, Chief of RAF Bomber Command: 'Congratulations from all ranks of Bomber Command on the highly successful completion of the first all-American raid by the big fellows on German-occupied territory in Europe. Yankee Doodle

certainly went to town and can stick yet another well-deserved feather in his cap.'

At the end of August a new AAF plan, AWPD/42, was issued to meet a Presidential request for a complete re-assessment of future air requirements. It was optimistic in its assumption that US bombers would enjoy low loss rates while inflicting high losses to the enemy fighters because of their superior fire-power. In essence AWPD/42 differed little from the original AWPD/1 but bombing priorities had shifted to the Atlantic U-boat pens because of the alarming losses of Allied shipping.

Unfortunately for Eaker, his ability to wage a bombing offensive was hampered by the more pressing needs of Brigadier General James H. Doolittle's 12th Air Force which would have to be equipped and trained to support the 'Torch' invasion of North West Africa in November 1942. The 8th Air Force was thus denied valuable replacement men and machines while new groups had to be trained for eventual transfer to the 12th. Worse, on 14 September both the 97th and 301st Bomb Groups were assigned to the new air force.

Meanwhile, Eaker sent all he had got on missions to shipyards and airfields on the continent. On 5 September 37 B-17s from the 97th and 301st Bomb Groups were despatched and the next day the 92nd helped swell the ranks to fifty-four. Despite their Spitfire escort two B-17s were shot down; the first US heavy bombers to be lost in the European Theatre of Operations (ETO). The 92nd later formed the first combat crew replacement centre.

Seventeen Liberators of the 93rd Bomb Group arrived at Alconbury in Huntingdonshire in September 1942 but the group remained in the shadow of Fortress operations for some time. From September to November four new B-17F bomb groups joined the 8th Air Force. It fell to these four B-17 Groups and two B-24 groups (in October 1942 the 93rd was joined by the 44th Bomb Group), to prove conclusively that daylight precision bombing could succeed in the deadly skies over Europe. The RAF remained unconvinced and even American instructors doubted their crew's ability to survive against German opposition.

The 305th Bomb Group was commanded by Lt Colonel Curtis E. LeMay, a man destined to figure prominently in the shaping of bombing doctrine both in the ETO and later, in the Pacific. On 9 October Eaker was able to despatch an unprecedented 108 bombers (including B-24Ds of the 93rd Bomb Group and B-17Fs of the 306th, both of which were making their bombing debuts), to Lille. A strong P-38 and RAF Spitfire escort accompanied the bombers. This first full scale mission created many problems, which coupled with bad weather, saw only sixty-nine bombers drop their bombs on the target area. Claims by the American gunners far exceeded the number of attacking enemy fighters but in fact the Luftwaffe lost just two.

Bombers against U-Boats

Allied shipping losses rose dramatically in October and November was to be even worse. On 20 October Brigadier General Asa N. Duncan, chief of Air Staff, issued a revised set of objectives to be carried out by VIII Bomber Command. In part it stated, '. . . Until

further orders every effort of the VIII Bomber Command will be directed to obtaining the maximum destruction of the submarine bases in the Bay of Biscay . . .' The limited number of Fortresses available prevented VIIIth Bomber Command hitting submarine yards inside Germany.

On 7 November 1942 the 44th Bomb Group flew its first mission when eight B-24Ds flew a diversionary sweep for B-17s attacking positions in Holland. Two days later twelve B-24s of the 44th and 93rd Bomb Groups went to Saint Nazaire in France to bomb the submarine pens.

The Liberator was not well suited to the ETO, mainly because on missions it was expected to conform to the performance limitation imposed by the Fortress. The B-24D's operationally high wing loading made it a difficult aircraft to maintain in formation above 21,000 feet although its service ceiling was put at 28,000 feet, about 4,000 feet below the optimum Fortress altitude. In addition, the B-24D's operational cruising speed of 180 mph was between ten and twenty miles per hour faster than the B-17s. This caused countless problems in mission planning and usually the Liberators were relegated to the rear of the B-17 formations where they consequently soaked up most of the punishment. The problem was that the B-17 was used in greater numbers and the B-24s had to adapt to the operational performance of the B-17 rather than the other way around.

Losses throughout the remainder of 1942 during missions to the U-boat pens were high although the planners still believed that the bombers could fight their way through to their objectives without fighter escort. The theory was given further credence on 20 December when only six B-17s from the attacking force of 101 bombers were lost on the mission to Romilly

Douglas A-20 Havoc light bombers were among the first US aircraft to arrive in England in the summer of 1942. *(US Air Force)*

near Paris despite widespread Luftwaffe fighter activity in France. Romilly was a turning point in the daylight aerial war. For the first time the Fortresses had penetrated 100 miles into enemy territory and had successfully kept the Luftwaffe interceptors at Bay (despite high claims, the American gunners actually shot down three and damaged one more).

One fact alarmed Eaker and his staff. Only 72 of the attacking bombers had hit the target and these caused only minimal damage. As improvements, some of them temporary until the new B-17Gs with 'chin turrets' to counter head-on attacks, came off the assembly lines, senior officers worked on methods for improving bombing and aerial gunnery. Lt. Colonel Curtis LeMay worked hard to find the best method of defense against fighter interceptions without compromising bombing accuracy and vice-versa. LeMay had faith in tight knit group formations and trained his men hard in very close formation flying.

At first LeMay experimented with 'stacked up' formations of eighteen aircraft, before he finally adopted staggered three-plane elements within a squadron and staggered squadrons within a group. At the same time LeMay discarded the traditional individual bombing and replaced the technique with 'lead crews'. The most expert bombardiers were placed in the lead crews. When the lead bombardier dropped his bombs so did everyone else. Providing he was on target all bombs landed near the MPI (Mean Point of Impact), and the target could be successfully destroyed instead of damaged. Eventually, lead crews, made up of highly trained pilots, bombardiers and navigators, became Standard Operating Procedure (SOP).

Group bombing was first tried on 3 January 1943 when the 8th Air Force visited Saint Nazaire for the sixth time. A total of 107 bombers, with the 305th of Curtis LeMay in the lead, was despatched but only eight B-24s and sixty-eight B-17s found the target. LeMay's tactics also called for a straight and level bomb run to ensure accuracy but seven bombers were shot down and forty-seven damaged, two so seriously that they were written off after landing in Wales. Most important of all, the majority of the bombloads had fallen into the pens.

Despite this first success, the future of 8th Bomber Command as a daylight bombing force was still in doubt. Losses had continued to rise and in some quarters (particularly the RAF) senior officers believed that the B-17s and B-24s should join the RAF night offensive. General Arnold, Chief of the American Air Staff, was under pressure from his superiors to mount more missions and in particular, aim them at German targets.

In January 1943 General Ira C. Eaker, who since November 1942 had been acting Commanding-General of the 8th Air Force in the absence of General Carl Spaatz (who had taken over all US African air commands), met General Arnold at the Casablanca summit in North Africa attended by President Roosevelt, Prime Minister Winston Churchill and the combined heads of staff, to make a case for continued daylight bombing.

Churchill had obtained an agreement from Roosevelt for the Eighth Air force to cease daylight bombing and join the RAF in night bombing. Eaker saw Churchill and managed to convince him otherwise. Churchill was most impressed with Eaker's brief memorandum which skillfully summarised the reasons why the US daylight bombing should continue. He particularly liked the phrase 'round the clock bombing' and although not totally convinced, was persuaded that day and night bombing be continued for a time.

To demonstrate that daylight precision bombing could triumph over area bombing by night Eaker decided to bomb the U-boat construction yards at Wilhelmshaven. On 27 January ninety-one B-17s and B-24s were despatched to the U-boat yards in the port. Unfortunately, bad weather conditions reduced the attacking force to fifty-three B-17s, which dropped their bombs on the shipyards from 25,000 feet through a German smoke screen and two others bombed Emden. Despite heavy fighter opposition only three bombers (one B-17 and two B-24s) were shot down. The bombing was described as 'fair' but the Press went wild.

The German defenses were constantly improving. Although flak (Flieger Abwehr Kannonen) accounted for most of the battle damage sustained by the B-17s and B-24s, the Luftwaffe continued to inflict the heaviest losses despite having only 200 fighters based in France and Low Countries. The 8th on the other hand, increased in strength. In April four new groups equipped with the B-17F (all but one group's aircraft were fitted with long-range 'Tokyo tanks') landed in England. A fifth 'new' B-17 group was added to the force when the 92nd Bomb Group resumed bombing operations.

As the Eighth penetrated ever deeper into the heart of the Reich its escort fighters were found wanting. The RAF Spitfires had no more than a 150 mile radius of action and almost all P-38F twin-engined fighters had been sent to North Africa. The 56th and 78th Fighter Groups had been operational on the P-47C and P-47D since February 1943 but teething troubles prevented their inaugural mission being flown until 13 April 1943. Even so, they only had a radius of action of 175 miles without auxiliary tanks.

Meanwhile, the 'heavies' continued to defend themselves while problems and protracted experiments involving various types of auxiliary drop tanks were carried out. On 4 May 1943 six squadrons of P-47s flew their first escort mission when the 56th Fighter Group, and six RAF fighter squadrons, accompanied 79 B-17s

THE EUROPEAN AIR WARS

The 78th Fighter Group based at Duxford Air Base, near Cambridge, received its Republic P-47C Thunderbolts in April 1943. P-47C 'El Jeepo' was the personal aircraft of Charles London, who was the first Fighter Ace of the 8th Air Force. Six Swastikas are visible just below the cockpit, representing six kills on German aircraft. *(US Air Force)*

to the Ford and General Motors plant at Antwerp. No bombers were lost.

On 12 May the 94th, 95th and 96th Bomb Groups formed a new Fourth Bomb Wing in Essex and Suffolk under the command of Brigadier General Fred L. Anderson. On 14 May Eaker was able to muster in excess of 200 bombers for the first time when 224 B-17s and B-24s and B-26 Marauder medium bombers attacked four separate targets. In a curtain raiser to the

day's events the Marauders flew low over Holland at roof-top height and bombed an electrical generating station at IJmuiden with delayed action mines.

About an hour later B-17s of the Wing, flying without escort, bombed the shipyards at Kiel. To the rear, Liberators of the 44th Bomb Group, which carried incendiaries, had to zig-zig all the way across the North Sea to maintain the slower speed of the Fortresses. By the time the coast was reached the B-24s were down to 18,000 feet and 100 mph: almost stalling speed. The 44th fell easy victim to the enemy flak and fighters and five B-24s were shot down before they had even dropped their bombs.

With two extra underwing tanks the Lockheed P-38 Lightning (here a P-38J of the 55th Fighter Group) was able to reach cities such as Hanover and Frankfurt. *(US Air Force)*

On 17 August Brigadier General Robert Williams, commander of the First Wing, led his force to Schweinfurt while Colonel Curtis E. LeMay led the 4th Wing to Regensburg. To minimise attacks from enemy fighters the master plan called for LeMay's force to fly on to North Africa after the target. The First Wing, meanwhile, would fly a parallel course to Schweinfurt to further confuse the enemy defences and return to England after the raid.

Unfortunately, the 1st Wing was delayed in England by ground mists, leaving the Luftwaffe time to concentrate on the 4th Wing and only one of four P-47 groups assigned to the 4th Wing actually managed to rendezvous with B-17s. They could not possibly cover all the seven B-17 groups, which stretched for fourteen miles. Enemy fighters ripped the formation apart and shot down twenty-four B-17s. The 1st Wing force fared worse, losing thirty-six B-17s to enemy fighters.

Those aircraft that had bombed had been remarkably accurate. Eighty hits were made on the factories at Schweinfurt and at Regensburg all six main workshops were destroyed or badly damaged. Air Marshal Slessor for the British, called it 'outstandingly successful, probably the best concentration on target yet seen'.

The official total of sixty B-17s lost was almost three times as high as the previous highest, on 13 June, when twenty-six bombers were lost. In reality the 8th had lost 147 bombers. Twenty-seven B-17s in the First Division were so badly damaged that they never flew again while sixty Fortresses had to be left in North Africa pending repairs. The almost non-existent maintenance facilities ruled out any further shuttle missions. The Luftwaffe made short shrift of the American bombers. The Germans taught a painful lesson; daylight bombing by heavy, relatively slow bombers without the protection of fast fighters was a strategic failure. The American Air Force licked its wounds and stayed out of German air space for nearly five weeks during which strategic bombing of German targets was left to the British Bomber Command.

VIII Bomber Command flew only shallow penetration missions throughout the remainder of August and early September 1943 while losses were made good. During September the B-17G, which introduced a 'chin turret' for forward defence, began arriving as combat replacements in the ETO. From November all new B-17 Groups arriving in England were similarly equipped.

In October the P-47's value as a long-range escort was proved when two jettisonable 150-gallon drop tanks were fitted below the wings which increased their range to over 300 miles from England. Even so, the Luftwaffe usually waited until the bombers were without their 'little friends' before engaging the bombers in combat.

Attacks have little effect

Despite the round-the-clock bombing of aircraft and component plants, British and American Intelligence sources estimated that the Luftwaffe had a first-line strength of between 1,525 and 1,100 single and twin-engined fighters respectively. In actuality, the Luftwaffe possessed 1,646 single and twin-engined fighters; considerably more than before the Pointblank directive had been issued. In an urgent response Eaker sent 291 B-17s to the ball bearing plants at Schweinfurt on 14 October in the hope that VIII Bomber Command could deliver a single, decisive blow to the German aircraft industry and stem the flow of fighters to Luftwaffe units.

Unfortunately, bad weather intervened before assembly, causing chaos in the B-17 formations and effectively preventing the Liberators of the Second Bomb Division from taking part in the mission. They were relegated, along with their fighter escort remnants, to a diversionary role over the North Sea. Vital fuel reserves aboard the B-17s were used up during long assembly procedures, made worse by cloudy conditions, while others were forced to abort with mechanical problems.

The fighter escorts did their best but bomber losses before the target were high. By the time it entered the target area the 1st Bomb Division had lost thirty-six bombers and twenty had turned back. The Third Division had lost only two bombers, leaving a total combined force of 227 B-17s, which hit their targets with remarkable effect.

To repel the attack on Schweinfurt, the Luftwaffe mobilized every fighter available for the Reichverteidigung, even bringing in fighter units from the Netherlands, Belgium and France. In his book *Der Luftkrieg über Deutschland*, the German author Franz Kurowski

The 49 pint-sized bombs painted on the fuselage of Marauder B-26C 'Mild and Bitter' represent 49 trips to enemy territory. This picture was taken while 'Mild and Bitter' was heading for target on its 50th mission. *(US Air Force)*

states that the German Air Force gathered itself for the most successful air battle of 1943 in which 300 Messerschmitt Bf 109 and Focke Wulf 190 'Tagjäger', forty Me 110 'Zerstörer' and around thirty Junkers Ju 88 'Nachtjäger' were involved. The German fighter pilots fell on their enemy with such unprecedented fury and took such a toll that American reports talked of 700 defending German fighters.

According to American author Martin Caidin in his gripping book *Black Monday*, the German fighter attacks were so fierce and so intense that the American B-17 crew members became desperate and distraught.

Duplication of claims during this extensive air battle resulted in American gunners claiming 189 German fighters shot down. The claims were whittled down to ninety-nine, or thirty-three per cent loss, but according to official German records only fifty fighters were lost. The 8th had lost sixty bombers, or nineteen per cent of its force. The 1st Bomb Division had lost forty-five B-17s and the Third Division, fifteen. Of the 231 bombers that returned to England 142 were damaged.

Despite the heavy damage caused by repeated air strikes, there was no appreciable reduction in German aircraft production. In this, the fourth year of the war, production, under the direction of Reichminister Albert Speer, even increased. In fact, in 1943, nearly 25,000 aircraft came off the production lines, equalling the total German aircraft production in the period 1939-1941. This rate of production helped Germany to make good its losses and remain at some sizeable strength. At the end of 1943, the German Air Force had around 1,500 fighters available for its defense in the west alone.

US Fighter Development

The day after the Schweinfurt raid, on 15 October, the 55th Fighter Group, equipped with the P-28H Lightning, saw combat for the first time. The 55th, and the 20th Fighter Group, which was also equipped with the P-38H, had arrived in England during August and September respectively. Although slightly slower and less manoeuvrable than most single-engined fighters then in service, the Lightning's greater range made it an excellent escort fighter. It could take a great deal of punishment, lose one engine and still get its pilot home.

Lightnings of the 20th Fighter Group first saw action on 28 December 1943. The 364th and 479th Fighter Groups followed in February and May 1944 respectively and flew their first missions on 3 March and 26 May 1944. The Ninth Tactical Air Force received the 367th, 370th and 374th Fighter Groups. The P-38J version which appeared in August 1943 carried two 165-gallon drop tanks which gave a combat range of 795 miles. During late 1944 five P-38 groups re-equipped with P-51s and one with the P-47. The 374th Fighter Group retained its P-38s until the end of the war.

Unfortunately, the Lightnings suffered from malfunctions caused by the unpredictable European weather and were often grounded. The one glimmer of hope for bomber crews was the introduction, late in 1943, of the North American P-51B Mustang, which could fly as far on its internal fuel as the P-47 could with drop tanks. Initially, the Mustang was introduced as a tactical fighter so the first deliveries of P-51Bs in November 1943 were assigned to three groups of the tactical 9th Air Force at the expense of VIIIth Fighter Command, whose need for a long-range escort fighter was critical. On 1 December 1943 P-51Bs of the 354th Fighter Group flew their first mission, a sweep over Belgium. The first escort mission for the bombers was not flown until 5 December.

A compromise was reached between the 8th and 9th Air Forces and the first 8th Air Force unit to receive the P-51B was the 357th Fighter Group, stationed at Raydon, Essex. They flew their first escort mission on 11 February 1944. In March 1944 P-51Bs flew to Berlin and back for the first time. Thenceforth the Mustang saw widespread use as an escort fighter on long-penetration raids deep into Germany. The Mustang's range of 2,080 miles, achieved by the use of wing drop tanks, was far in excess of that available in other fighters of the day. By the end of the war the P-51 equipped all but one of the 8th Air Force fighter groups.

In many aspects the P-51 was better than the German Bf 109 and Fw 190 fighters. The German pilots were suffering heavily because in air battle the Mustang was invincible. The P-51 pilots achieved their victories (kills) effortlessly and often the crews of the B-17 and B-24 bombers listening in on their radios heard distraught young German pilots screaming 'Mustang,

Top left: The Germans often released smoke screens in an effort to hide their industrial sites, harbours or railroad yards. In this picture, taken on 8 October 1943, Boeing B-17s fly over the target at Bremen, just prior to bomb release. *(US Air Force)*

Left: The smokescreens were not always effective. The picture shows the smokescreen the Nazis released to hide Wilhelmshaven (11 June 1943). The screen was, however, blown away by the wind over the sea. An industrial site can be clearly seen below left in the picture. *(US Air Force)*

Mustang' to their fellow pilots to warn them of an attack.

The 56th FG was unique in the 8th AF, choosing to retain its P-47s until the end of hostilities The 56th FG — the most famous fighter group of the 8th — was nicknamed Zemke's Wolf Pack after its commanding officer Colonel Hubert Zemke. The group arrived in England in April 1943 and on the 13th of the same month began operational flights. The Wolf Pack flew its last mission on 21st April 1945 by which time it had recorded no less than 674½ victories in the air and had also destroyed 311 aircraft on the ground. Many famous aces served with this unit including Colonel Hubert Zemke (17¾ confirmed kills in the air), Major Gerald W Johnson (with eighteen confirmed kills) and the top scoring fighter aces, Colonel Francis 'Gabby' Gabreski (who was the leading ace in the ETO with twenty-eight victories and 2½ strafing credits) and Major Robert Johnson (twenty-eight aerial victories).

Birth of the Strategic Air Force

In October 1943 the 9th Air Force was transferred from North Africa to England in order to build up a tactical air force for the invasion of Europe planned for the following spring. General Henry H. Arnold, meanwhile, had proposed a plan to split the 12th Air Force in two to create a Strategic Air Force in the Mediterranean, leaving the remaining half of the 12th as a tactical organization. The possibility of a Strategic Air Force based in southern Italy would effectively place parts of Austria, Germany and eastern Europe, previously out of range of the 8th Air Force, within easy reach. Italy also offered potentially better weather conditions than Britain.

Arnold's plan was accepted and on 1 November 1943 the 15th Air Force was officially activated with a strength of ninety B-24s and 210 B-17s, inherited from

A Focke-Wulf 190 attacks a Boeing B-17 on its way to bomb Bremen on 29 November 1943. *(US Air Force)*

the 12th Air Force. Initially, the two B-24 groups and four B-17 groups formed the operational element of the 15th Air Force, based at thirteen airfields in the Foggia-Cerignola area. By the end of the month another 201 Liberators were added. New groups, most of which were equipped with B-24s, soon started arriving from the United States. Starting in December 1943 the first of thirteen new Liberator groups joined the 15th Air Force.

On 4 January 1944 the B-24s and B-17s in England flew their last mission under the auspices of VIII Bomber Command. The 15th Air Force had now been established in Italy and it was decided to embrace both the 8th and 15th in a new headquarters, called US Strategic Air Forces, Europe, (USSTAF — the overall USAAF command organization in Europe) at Bushey Hall, Teddington, Middlesex, previously Headquarters, 8th Air Force. General Carl Spaatz returned to England to command the new organization while Major General Jimmy Doolittle relinquished command of the 15th to Major General Nathan F. Twining, and took over command of the 8th Air Force; its head-quarters moving to High Wycombe. Doolittle of course was well known to American airmen as the famous Tokyo leader and former air racer. His directive was simple: 'Win the air war and isolate the battlefield'.

Lieutenant General Ira C. Eaker was transferred to the Mediterranean theatre to take command of the new MAAF (Mediterranean Allied Air Forces). Eaker had built up the 8th Air Force from nothing and Churchill told him in January 1944, 'The predictions you made to me at Casablanca last February about our combined bomber missions, including "round the clock bombing" are now being verified. I no longer have any doubt that they will prove competely valid.'

A North American P-51B Mustang of the 354th Fighter Group. This 'Pioneer Mustang Group' was the first unit to receive the Mustang in December 1943. *(US Air Force)*

Spaatz and Doolittle's plan was to use the US Strategic Air Forces in a series of co-ordinated raids, code-named Operation 'Argument' and supported by RAF night bombing, on the German aircraft industry at the earliest possible date. As usual, the winter weather caused a series of postponements and the bombers were despatched meanwhile, to V1 rocket sites, or 'No-ball' targets, as they were known. Of the twenty-nine missions flown during January-February 1944, thirteen were to the ski-shaped targets in northern France.

'Big Week' offensive

Good weather was predicted for the week 20-25 February and so 'Operation Argument', which quickly became known as 'Big Week', began in earnest. The opening shots were fired by the RAF which bombed Leipzig on the night of 19-20 February. Meanwhile, both the 8th and 15th Air Forces were readied but the latter was committed to supporting the Anzio operation and did not take part on 20 February. The Eighth put up some 1,028 B-17s and B-24s and 832 fighters while the RAF provided sixteen squadrons of Mustangs and Spitfires. In all, twelve aircraft plants were attacked, with the B-17s of the First going to Leipzig, Bernburg and Oschersleben while the Liberators went to the Me 110 plants at Gotha. The unescorted Third Division bombed the Fw 190 plant at Tutow and the He 111 plant at Rostock.

The raids caused such widespread damage that it lead Speer to order the immediate dispersement of the German aircraft industry to safer parts of the Reich.

Next day 924 bombers and 679 fighters of the 8th Air Force set out for two aircraft factories at Brunswick and other targets. The 15th was grounded by bad weather in the Foggia area. H2X blind bombing equipment was used at Brunswick when heavy cloud prevented visual bombing and some groups bombed targets of opportunity. This time the 8th lost nineteen bombers and five fighters but claimed sixty German fighters shot down.

On 22 February it was intended that the 15th Air Force strike at Regensburg while the 8th struck at other targets in the Reich including Gotha and Schweinfurt but the majority of the 8th's bomb groups were forced to abort because of bad weather over England. The 15th despatched a force of 183 bombers to the Obertraubling Messerschmitt assembly plant Regensburg. Some 118 bombed with good results but fourteen were shot down. The 8th lost a staggering forty-one bombers.

On 23 February bad weather kept the 8th Air Force heavies on the ground but Twining's 15th Air Force sent 102 bombers to the Steyr ball-bearing works in Austria where they destroyed twenty per cent of the plant.

On the 24th Doolittle despatched 867 bombers to a wide range of targets in Germany. The First Division attacked Schweinfurt, losing eleven B-17s, while the Third Division struck at targets on the Baltic coast without any loss. Some 239 B-24s of the 2nd Bomb Division, which attacked the Me 110 assembly plant at Gotha, came off worst. Over 180 B-24s inflicted considerable damage to the plant but twenty-eight Liberators were shot down. Twining sent 114 B-17s and B-24s to Steyr again but the force became separated and the Liberators bombed their Fiume oil refinery instead. Seventeen bombers failed to return to Italy.

On 25 February the USSTAF brought the curtain down on Big Week when 1,300 8th and 15th Air force bombers and 1,000 fighters were despatched to aircraft plants, ball bearing works and components factories throughout the Reich. The First Bomb Division heavily damaged the Messerschmitt experimental and assembly plants at Augsburg and the VFK ball-bearing plants at Stuttgart were also hit.

The Second Bomb Division bombed the Me 110 components plant at Furth and very considerable damage was caused to the Me 109 plants at Regensburg by the Third Bomb Division and 176 bombers of the 15th Air Force. The latter force hit the aircraft plants an hour before the England-based force arrived over the city. Output at both Augsburg and Regensburg was severely reduced for four months following the raids. The 8th lost thirty-one bombers while the 15th Air Force lost thirty-three bombers.

Despite total losses during Big Week of some 226 bombers, Spaatz and Doolittle believed the USSTAF had dealt the German aircraft industry a really severe blow. In reality though, the destruction was not as great as at first thought.

Bombers over Berlin

Less than a week later, on 3 March 1944, the USSTAF launched its first attack on Berlin, the Reichshauptstadt of the Third Reich. However the attack was aborted because of bad weather and the following day only the 95th and 100th Bomb Groups of the Third Division defied the elements and dropped the first American bombs on 'Big-B'.

On 6 March the 8th despatched 730 heavies and almost 800 escort fighters to targets in Berlin and this time made it. A ball-bearing plant at Erkner in the suburbs of Berlin, the Robert Bosch Electrical Equipment factory and the Daimler Benz engine factory at Genshagen were all bombed. The American gunners claimed over 170 German fighters destroyed but the 8th lost a record sixty-three bombers with a further 102 seriously damaged and eleven fighters.

In 1944 many fighter groups converted to the North American P-51 Mustang. This P-51D, named 'Lou VI', belonged to the 361st Fighter Group. The aircraft is carrying a 400-litre drop tank under each wing. *(US Air Force)*

On 8 March all three divisions of the 8th Air Force contributed 600 bombers and 200 escort fighters in the raid on the VKF ball-bearing plant at Erkner. The leading Third Division received the worst of the fighter attacks and lost 37 Fortresses. The following day Berlin was covered by thick cloud, but this did not prevent the Americans from launching yet another new attack. Thanks to the total absence of the Luftwaffe the mission was still a success. Only nine bombers were lost to flak as they attempted to bomb Berlin through thick cloud. Reportedly the German fighters were kept on the ground because no one believed that the Americans were capable of precision bombing throughout heavy cloud cover. But the 8th used radar equipped bombers to find the targets. Altogether, the 8th Air Force dropped 4,800 tons of high explosive on Berlin during five raids in March 1944. On the 22 March raid on 'Big-B' 800 bombers were despatched, once again led by H2X-radar (code name 'Mickey Mouse') equipped B-17 and B-24 bombers of the 482nd Bomb Group. These 'pathfinders' proved, in fact, very capable of finding the targets and guiding the bombers to them. Thereafter, each bomb division had a PFF (Pathfinder Force) squadron of its own.

Prelude to Invasion

At Allied headquarters in England, several months of feverish activity had already gone into planning the large scale invasion of continental Europe. Early in 1944 it was decided that Operation 'Overlord' would take place on the Normandy beaches in France. Opposition from German tank divisions in the area was to be expected so, to weaken resistance as much as possible, it was necessary for supply lines in the hinterland to be attacked so that provisioning was delayed. German mobility would also stagnate if fuel

supplies were disrupted.

In a prelude to the invasion American air attacks began in February 1944 against railway junctions, airfields, ports and bridges in northern France and the Atlantic coastline. Fighters from the 8th, 9th and 12th Air Forces mounted strafing missions called 'Jackpot' (aimed at airfields) and 'Chattanooga Choo-Choo' (primarily aimed at rail networks). Within four months Allied fighter pilots had succeeded in destroying, or severely damaging, hundreds of locomotives, thousands of goods wagons and vehicles and tens of bridges. German airfields in France and Belgium were hit too.

In April overall command of the Combined Bomber Offensive and the 8th Air Force officially passed to General Dwight D. Eisenhower, newly appointed Supreme Allied Commander, Allied Expeditionary Forces (SHAEF). Coincidentally, that same month Generalmajor Adolf Galland, the Luftwaffe fighter commander, revealed to his superiors that since January his day fighter arm had lost more than 1,000 pilots. He estimated that each Allied air raid was costing the Luftwaffe about fifty aircrew. If this continued Galland said the time was fast approaching when the Luftwaffe would lose air control over Germany.

May Day marked the opening of a series of all-out attacks from England on the enemy's rail network in support of the Pointblank directive, when 1,328 Eighth Air Force bombers struck at targets in France and Belgium. On 7 May, 1,000 American heavies were despatched for the first time and two days later 772 bombers attacked transportation targets. On 11 May 973 bombers bombed marshalling yards in Germany and the Low Countries.

By June 1944 the 15th Air Force was bombing railway networks in south-east Europe in support of Russian military operations in Rumania. Throughout the summer of 1944 Austrian aircraft manufacturing centres at Wiener Neustadt were bombed and oil producing centres too, were attacked. Although the Eighth Air Force was heavily committed to pre-invasion attacks on enemy lines of communication, in an attempt to meet both transportation and oil objectives it continued to bomb both types of target right up until D-Day, 6 June.

On this momentous day Liberators of the Second Bomb Division led the 8th Air Force on the first of three strikes on the Normandy and Cherbourg invasion areas, each aimed at neutralising enemy coastal defenses and front-line troops. Altogether, 2,362 bomber sorties were flown on D-Day, for the loss of only three B-24s.

In July the 15th began 'softening up' targets in southern France in preparation for the invasion code-named, 'Anvil'. Marseilles, Lyon, Grenoble and Toulon all felt the weight of bombs dropped by the B-24s and B-17s.

The Luftwaffe was notable by its absence and the Allied air forces continued to dominate the skies over Europe. On 2 June the 15th Air Force had flown its first 'shuttle' mission when 130 B-17s and P-51 escorts had landed in Russia after a raid on Hungary. Two more 15th Air Force 'shuttle' missions followed and then on 21 June the Eighth flew its first 'shuttle' mission, bombing Berlin and landing at Poltava, Russia. Following the mission 43 B-17s and several P-51s were destroyed in an audacious attack carried out by the Luftwaffe. The experience did not prevent the 8th from flying three more 'shuttle' missions during August-September 1944.

Ford-built B-24H Liberator of the 392nd Bombardment Group arrived at Wendling, Norfolk, in August 1944. *(US Air Force)*

Oil Production bears the brunt

In April General Eisenhower had ordered USSTAF to attack German fuel production centres by striking both the oil refineries and the factories producing synthetic fuels; the Achilles heel of the German war machine. The 15th Air Force had started the offensive on 5 April when it despatched 235 B-24s and B-17s from Italy to transportation targets in the vicinity of the Ploesti oilfields in Rumania. Although the Americans did not officially admit to starting an oil offensive, the Ploesti refineries were again bombed on 15 and 24 April, causing 'incidental' damage.

The Eighth Air Force did not strike at oil targets until 12 May when 900 bombers, escorted by over 875 fighters, pounded oil targets in the Leipzig area (Zeitz, Böhlen, Lützen and Merseburg/Leuna) and at Brüx (Most) in Czechoslovakia. A smaller force attacked a Fw 190 repair depot at Zwickau. Over the target areas the bombers were attacked by 300 German fighters which attacked with well known ferocity. At a cost of almost half its aircraft, the German Jagdverbande succeeded in shooting down forty-six bombers and ten fighters in an unequal fight.

Attacks on oil targets had assumed top priority by the autumn of 1944 but the refineries were dispersed throughout the four corners of the Reich so a concentrated and effective offensive proved difficult. Nevertheless, vast aerial fleets of 8th and 15th Air Force B-24s and B-17s escorted by P-51s and P-38s, bombed oil refineries in Germany, Czechoslovakia and Rumania during late 1944-early 1945. Total air superiority meant that the USSTAF could roam far and wide throughout the Greater Reich, hitting targets as

Above: Berlin after the war: the result of the area bombing by the British Bomber Command. German cities like Hamburg, Cologne, Frankfurt and Dresden were totally destroyed after almost non-stop bombing in the last month. *(Landesbildstelle Berlin)*

Right: The result of a 'Jackpot'-run: a badly damaged Fw 190 at the Belgian airfield Melsbroek, near Brussels.

far afield as Ploesti in Rumania, Brüx in Czechoslovakia, Budapest, Komorom, Gyor and Petfurdo in Hungary, Belgrade and other cities in Yugoslavia and Trieste in north-eastern Italy.

The Merseburg GmbH refineries in Leuna, where the majority of synthetic fuel for Germany's rocket powered fighters was manufactured, was attacked on at least eighteen occasions in 1944. On the final raid, on 30 November, twenty-nine bombers and forty fighters were shot down. The attacks on Merseburg only reduced daily production to a mere ten per cent of normal but at the end of 1944 only three out of ninety-one refineries in the Reich were still working normally; twenty-nine were partly operational and the remainder were out of action for months.

Post D-Day missions

On 20 August the 20th Wing of the 8th Air Force converted to a transportation role in support of the Allied ground forces in France, who were in urgent need of fuel and supplies. On 29 August the Liberators of the 93rd, 446th and 448th Bomb Groups commenced 'trucking' missions, as they were called. These missions continued until 9 September but then the Allies launched Operation 'Market Garden' using British and American airborne divisions against German-held Dutch towns on the Rhine.

In mid-September the B-24s were once again called upon to supplement the troop carriers. On 12 September the 458th Bomb Group from Horsham St. Faith delivered just over 13,000 gallons of fuel to units in France. Altogether, 252 supply-carrying B-24s took off for France on the first full divisional 'trucking' mission on 18 September, including six specially modified Liberators from the 458th, delivering over 9,000 gallons of fuel to General Patton's forces. During September, in thirteen days of flying 'trucking' missions, the 458th alone delivered 727,160 gallons of fuel to France.

On 27 September the Liberators of the 2nd Bomb Division got back to the bombing war with sad results. A total of 315 B-24s were despatched to the Henschel engine and vehicle assembly plants at Kassel in central Germany. Mistakes cost the 445th Bomb Group dearly and twenty-five of its thirty-seven B-24s despatched were shot down in fierce fighter attacks. Losses within the division as a whole continued to rise and on 25 November the 491st Bomb Group lost sixteen B-24s in almost as many minutes during a mission to oil refineries at Mieburg, Hanover.

51

A question of Time

Late in 1944 Hitler had planned one last major offensive against the allied armies along the French-Belgian border. On 16 December, using the appalling weather conditions to his advantage, Field Marshal Karl von Rundstedt and his panzer formations attacked American positions in the forests of the Ardennes and opened up a salient or 'Bulge' in the Allied lines. In England the Allied air forces were grounded by fog and it was not until 23 December that the heavies could offer bomber support in the 'Battle of the Bulge'. On Christmas Eve a record 2,034 8th Air Force bombers and 500 RAF and 9th Air Force bombers, took part in the largest single strike flown by the Allied Air Forces in World War Two, against German airfields and lines of communication leading to the 'Bulge'.

In January 1945 the Luftwaffe attempted one last major air offensive against the Allied air forces. Since 20 December many Jagdgeschwader had been transferred to airfields in the west for Operation 'Bodenplatte'. Precisely how many fighters the Luftwaffe managed to bring to bear is unknown. The German historian, Frans Kurowski, in his book *Der Luftkrieg über Deutschland* says 850 fighters.

At 07.45 hours on Sunday morning 1 January, the German fighter force took off and attacked twenty-seven airfields in northern France, Belgium and southern Holland. After four hours of battle, most of the allied airfields were severely damaged and a large number of aircraft had been destroyed. Success at a price. Operation Bodenplatte cost the already weak Luftwaffe 300 aircraft, most of which were shot down by Allied anti-aircraft guns.

The end comes in sight

Operation Bodenplatte was supposed to be a great wave. Instead it was just a ripple. It was the writing on the wall; the German Ardennes offensive was a total failure. For Germany, like King Canute, there remained only hopeless attempts to turn the tide. Me 262 jet fighters could still be expected to put in rare attacks and during March almost all enemy fighter interceptions of American bombers were made by the Jagdverbände.

On 2 March, when the bombers were despatched to synthetic oil refineries at Leipzig, Me 262s attacked near Dresden. The following day the largest formation of German jets ever seen made attacks on 8th Air Force bomber formations heading for Dresden and oil targets at Ruhrland and shot down three heavies.

But Germany's 'wonder weapons' had been developed too late and too few Me 262 jet fighters and Me 163 Komet rocket aircraft were available in 1945 to stave off German defeat. The V1 and V2 rocket sites were gradually overrun and lack of fuel and suitable pilots had virtually driven the Luftwaffe from German skies. In the air, however, the Me 262 was still an elusive foe for the American fighters. It represented the latest generation of fighters against which the piston-engined-powered P-47 and P-51 could not compete. On the ground, however, this advanced jet fighter was as paralysed as a 50-ton locomotive. So in the final phase of the war, the Americans concentrated on bombing and ground strafing particularly of airfields where Me 262s were stationed. One such raid took place on

21 March when the 15th Air Force despatched 366 Liberators to the jet factory and airfield at Neuburg. The attack was carried out visually and the plant was almost completely destroyed. Three days later 271 B-24s finished off the job, destroying twenty-five jets on the airfield in the process. On 27 March 12th Air Force P-47 Thunderbolts strafed Lechfeld airfield in Bavaria and destroyed large numbers of German jet aircraft.

On 24 March the 15th Air Force bombed Berlin for the first time and by the end of the month the strategic offensive was almost over. The Luftwaffe was prepared to do anything to stop the stream of bombers and in their desperation even went so far as to use so-called 'Rammjäger'; converted Bf 109 fighters flown by suicide pilots from Sonderkommando Elbe. On 7 April, the Luftwaffe for the first time employed Rammjäger in the fight against American bomber streams attacking underground oil refineries in central Germany. During their ramming attacks the suicide commandos were protected by Me 262s. The Rammjäger dived into the bomber formations from a height of 33,000 feet before destroying twenty-three aircraft. Altogether, seventy-seven German pilots lost their lives during suicide attacks against the American bomber formations.

Next day the Eighth despatched thirty-two B-17 and B-24 groups and fourteen Mustang groups to targets in Germany. On 9 and 10 April the German jet airfields were again bombed. On the latter mission a record 297 German aircraft were destroyed on the ground by fighters employing ground strafing attacks. On 16 April this record was broken when just over 700 aircraft were destroyed. The Luftwaffe was finished.

The biggest 15th Air Force operation of all occurred on 15 April when 1,235 bombers were despatched to Wowser near Bologna. The last major air battle took place on 18 April when 305 B-17s and 906 B-24s, plus more than 1,200 fighters, were sent to attack Berlin. Jagdgeschwader 7 'Hindenburg' had managed to assemble approximately forty Me 262s and they tore into the 8th and 15th Air Force formations. The Messerschmitts were far too fast for the American P-51, which did not have a snowflake's chance in hell against them. Even the ridiculously large number of 1,200 fighters was not enough to stop the Messerschmitts, only two of which were shot down by the American P-51s. The Me 262s, however, managed to shoot down twenty-five bombers with rockets.

During the week 18-25 April missions were briefed and scrubbed almost simultaneously. The end came on 25 April 1945 when 8th Air Force flew its last full-scale mission of the war. While B-17s bombed the Skoda armaments factory at Pilsen in Czechoslovakia, Liberators of the Second Air Division bombed four rail complexes surrounding Hitler's mountain retreat at Berchtesgaden. The 15th Air Force, meanwhile, prevented German troops escaping from Italy by bombing lines of communication in Austria and the Brenner Pass.

When the Germans in Italy finally surrendered, on 2 May, the heavies in the 15th Air Force joined the 8th Air Force in dropping supplies and evacuating Allied prisoners of war. Groups from England flew 'Trolly' missions over western Europe so that ground crews could witness at first hand the considerable destruction their charges had wrought.

Chapter 3
Peace: jet fighters and atom bombs

After the German Army's unconditional surrender on 8 May 1945, the disarmament of the Luftwaffe was one of the most important tasks of the US Army Air Forces. The Luftwaffe's elimination was carried out vigorously. Reasonable numbers of the newer types of aircraft, such as the Messerschmitt Me 262 and the Heinkel He 162 Volkjäger jet fighter, were discovered on the airfields around München and these were shipped to America for further inspection. The same happened to materials discovered at the air bases of several Luftwaffe Erprobungskommandos. At the Lechfeld air base near Augsburg, for example, not only were large numbers of Me 262 jet fighters discovered but also valuable German air-to-air rockets. And at the Oberpfaffenhofen air base near München the Americans managed to lay their hands on the high-speed Dornier Do 335 Pfeil. This Dornier was powered by two twelve-cylinder 1,800 horsepower Daimler-Benz engines with which the Do 335, rightly nicknamed the 'Arrow', reached a speed of 760 km/h — just one hundred kilometres slower than the maximum speed of the Me 262 jet fighter.

The remainder of the Luftwaffe's equipment awaited the breaker's hammer and scrapper's furnace.

Demobilization

Shortly after the end of the war, the Americans, who were still actively demolishing the Luftwaffe, also began to demobilize most of their own Air Force. At that moment the US Strategic Air Forces in Europe (USSAFE) commanded around 17,000 aircraft and an organization made up of around half a million men. Many 'Airmen' and much of the flying materials were transferred to the Pacific theatre.

The aim was to maintain just a small organization in Europe, exclusively for communication and transport purposes. 'All I require is an Air Force of about 7,500 personnel to provide transport and communications,' said the European theatre commander General Joseph T. McNarny, according to the official American version. Evidently General Dwight D. Eisenhower, Commander of the American armed forces, at whom McNarny's proclamation was aimed, thought exactly the same way. This is indicated by his August 1945 order for the word 'strategic' to be removed from the US Strategic Air Forces in Europe. Eisenhower, apparently, considered there was no longer any need for a strategic American force in Europe. On 7 August

1945 his order was carried out: the US Air Forces in Europe (USAFE) was then a fact.

In September 1945, USAFE headquarters moved from Paris to Luisenstrasse 13 in Wiesbaden, Germany, from where the continued demobilization of the Air Force was organized. By the end of 1946 the American Air Force in Europe comprised only around 75,000 men and less than 2,000 aircraft.

The Polish question

The optimism of the military command was in sharp contrast to political developments in Europe at the time. American-Russian differences which, paradoxically, appeared negligible during the war when they were fighting a common enemy, came to the fore again in 1945. The basis for the differences originated at Yalta in February 1945 during a summit conference between the Big Three (America, Russia and Britain). Yalta was the last in a series of summit conferences and followed Casablanca, Quebec, Moscow and Teheran. It was also the most important meeting between the Big Three in wartime. During the Yalta conference Roosevelt, Churchill and Stalin discussed post-war borders, set German reparation payments and decided to occupy the whole of Germany. Berlin, the former capital of the Third Reich, and Germany itself, were divided into occupation zones. Germany was roughly divided geographically into a western zone and an eastern zone. The eastern zone was Russia's while the western zone was divided between America and Britain. Berlin, which lay in the Russian zone, was also divided in this way. Later, France, which had vainly asked to participate in the Yalta summit, was granted occupation zones in Germany and Berlin which were formed out of the American and British occupation zones.

One of the core problems during the Yalta conference was Poland. The 'Polish question' was to become a large stumbling block in the relationships between the Allies. As far as the Russians were concerned the matter was simple: Poland, had in the past attacked Russia more than once, and must be brought into the Russian sphere of influence. Poland's borders must be redrawn and the new Polish government must be unequivocally pro-Russian. The Western Allies, rightly, continued to press for democratic government and free elections. Russia also laid claim to a large area of Polish territory. A compromise seemed impossible. Russia's power position was clear: the Red Armies had liberated Poland and, therefore, Poland's future was a matter for the Russians to decide.

De-mobilisation in June 1945. North American P-51 Mustangs of the 78th Fighter Group line up on Duxford Air Base, England. Most of these fighters went back to the United States. Also many were used to re-arm the western air forces. *(US Air Force)*

The 'Casey Jones' project

Shortly after World War 2, the US Air Force began a series of reconnaissance flights over Europe that led to numerous skirmishes and high tension. During the war, the American photographic and observation Groups in England regularly carried out photo flights over Germany. These reconnaissance flights not only provided American Fighter Command with a clear picture of the bomb damage sustained by German industry but also enabled strategic German targets to be put on the map.

American aerial espionage did not stop once the war in Europe was over. On the contrary, in the second half of 1945 the number of reconnaissance flights increased. Within this framework the USAFE's task changed from strategic bombing — unnecessary since Germany's surrender — to air intelligence and aerial mapping. Between the autumn of 1945 and the summer of 1947, the USAFE carried out a series of projects, during which areas in west and central Europe, North Africa and the Atlantic islands were mapped for future military use.

The first project in the series was codenamed 'Casey Jones'. Among the aircraft used were RB-24L Liberators and RB-17F Flying Fortresses (originally designated F-7 and F-9 respectively). These were converted bombers fitted with a large number of cameras. Casey Jones reconnaissance flights were only supposed to be flown over the Western Allies' occupation zones but the American Information Service has never released any information about these flights and there is a strong suspicion that the reconnaissance aircraft also operated over the Russian occupation zone. There are indications that the Central Intelligence Group — the American secret service established in January 1946 and renamed the Central Intelligence Agency (CIA) in 1947 — was

involved in the aerial mapping. The American Secret Service had a Cartographic Information Department right from the beginning.

According to Dick J. Burkard, historian of the USAF Military Airlift Command, in 1946 the Air Transport Command (ATC) had 33 Douglas C-47 'Gooney Birds' in Europe and the Pacific area that were used for Special Operations missions. Did the American Secret Service use these C-47s for flights over Russian territory?

It is very likely, as the numerous skirmishes between American and Russian aircraft indicate. Russian fighters regularly opened fire on American craft caught over the Russian occupation zones and time and again it was the ATC C-47s that were involved. On 22nd April 1946, for example, an American C-47 near the Tulln air base near Vienna (which, like Berlin was under joint Allied control) was attacked by Russian Air Force Bell P-39 Airacobra fighters. On 9 August Yugoslavian fighters opened fire on a C-47 and forced it to land. According to American reports, a navigational error took the C-47, which was *en route* to Udine air base in Italy, off course and over Yugoslavian territory.

Ten days later there was another clash and coincidentally (?), it was another ATC C-47 that was flying over Yugoslavian territory because of a navigational error. This time the C-47 was shot down by Yugoslavian fighters.

Truman loses patience

Obviously Poland was not the only bone of contention between America and Russia. There were many more. The Western Allies were particularly agitated by the Russian expansionist drive in Bulgaria and Rumania and also threatened Hungary. Moreover, in violation of the agreement with the Allies, Russian troops still occupied Iran and the Russians were putting political pressure on Turkey and Greece in order to gain control of the Dardanelles and a passage to the Near East from the Black Sea.

The Russian expansion formed the basis of Churchill's speech on 5 March 1946 in Fulton, Missouri, where he spoke of an 'Iron Curtain' being drawn from Stettin on the Baltic to Trieste on the Adriatic. President Truman had also warned of the Russian menace shortly after the war. 'I do not doubt for a moment that Russia will attack Turkey,' he told James Byrnes, his advisor and Minister of Foreign Affairs. Henceforth Truman wanted to take a hard line with Russia, lest the situation led irrevocably to a new war. He wanted no more compromises. He refused to ackowledge Rumania and Bulgaria, demanded Russian troops leave Iran immediately and forced Russia to an agreement over the payment of Lend-Lease debts. Truman was 'tired of babying the Soviets'.

America shows the flag

Truman re-formed the American fleet and stationed most of the vessels in the Mediterranean. The Americans also held onto their forward bases in Iceland which placed their bombers just 3,000 kilometers from Leningrad and Moscow. In Germany, former Luftwaffe airfields such as Fürstenfeldbruck near München, Giebelstadt near Würzburg and Rhein Main near Frankfurt were rebuilt so that Boeing B-29 Super-fortresses loaded with atom bombs could be stationed there.

The B-29 heavy bomber used in the nuclear attacks on Hiroshima and Nagasaki that ended World War 2, was back in production as the B-29D (soon to be redesignated the B-50 Superfortress) which had a range

RB-24L reconnaissance aircraft were converted from Liberator heavy bombers. This type was used to carry out Casey Jones reconnaissance missions. Cameras were mounted in the nose section and in the bomb bay. *(Smithsonian Institution)*.

of nearly 7,000 kilometers. Preparations were also made for the production of the Convair B-36, a giant intercontinental bomber that would permit SAC to reach targets deep in the Russian heartland from bases in the US.

In his book *Der Kalte Krieg*, the German commentator Wolfgang Kahn wrote that the American strategists wanted to station the SAC B-29s as close to the Soviet Union as possible because of their limited range. Permanent stationing at American bases in Germany was at hand.

In November 1946 the time had come: to help oil the wheels of diplomacy, six B-29s from the SAC's 43rd Bombardment Group were sent to Rhein Main air base in Germany. From there the bombers visited various bases in England, France, Turkey and Greece (the latter for 'flag showing' patrol flights along Russian and Bulgarian borders). In May 1947 Strategic Air Command stationed a number of B-29s in Germany at Giebelstadt and Fürstenfeldbruck. This series of so-called 'training deployments' was intended to give SAC pilots the opportunity of gaining flight experience in Europe. To keep up the pretence of a training programme the B-29 Units were continuously exchanged with Squadrons from the US. These deployments were only a cover-up. The aim was to have a strategic air force permanently stationed in Europe.

'Extraversion'

At the beginning of 1945, the first American jet fighters were secretly shipped to Europe. They were four prototypes of the Lockheed YP-80A Shooting Star jet fighter which were tested under operational conditions in Europe under the code-name 'Extraversion'. In the *Encyclopaedia of US Air Force Aircraft and Missile Systems*, officially published by the US Office of Air force History, the American historian Marcelle Size Knack wrote that the Extraversion lasted for three months and took place mainly in the Mediterranean region. It may be assumed that bases in Italy and North Africa were used for this test programme because of the good weather in these areas. It may also be assumed, although it has never been officially confirmed, that the Lockheed jets took part in the US Air Force air operations and there are indications that they put in a respectable performance.

The four Extraversion YP-80s were from a series of thirteen prototypes Lockheed supplied to the Air Force

for evaluation purposes. One YP-80 went to the National Advisory Committee for Aeronautics (NACA) for speed tests and another was converted into an XF-14 reconnaissance aircraft. As usual the rest went to the Air Force Flight Test Center at Muroc in California for evaluation. Muroc Dry Lake is now known as Edwards Air Force Base. The Extraversion YP-80s really were an exception: they were sent to Europe on tactical duty which implied that they, in fact, came under the jurisdiction of the USSAFE. Would the USSAFE have hesitated for one moment at the chance to operationally test America's latest jet fighter and to put it through its paces? It is also unlikely that the P-80s only made good weather flights in Europe; if good weather was a criterion they would have stayed in California. At the end of May 1945 two YP-80s crashed for reasons unkown and shortly afterwards the Extraversion project was stopped. The two remaining YP-80s were sent back to the US.

★   ★   ★

Above: A Douglas C-47 of the Air Transport Command strayed over the Yugoslavian border and was promptly attacked by Yugoslavian fighters. *(DoD)*

Left: The Boeing B-29 went into production again. The B-29D version (later re-named B-50) had new engines, a greater wingspan, a higher tail and had an operational range of nearly seven thousand kilometers. *(Boeing)*

one reason was the pilots' inexperience with fast jet fighters. In 1946, just as in 1945, the P-80s were not a success in Europe. Because of lack of parts, operations and maintenance became a problem, and the jets were shipped out of the command by year's end.

The Truman Doctrine

On 12 March 1947, in an address before the American Congress, President Truman sketched a portrait of a world divided in two: a democratic free half and a half that was not free but which lived under a communist regime. He stressed that every country in the world must choose between the two systems but that too often it would not be a free choice. The crux of his argument was American aid for countries threatened by communism. It was a direct answer to Marxist-Leninist ideology, the basis of the communist 'world revolution' so feared by the Americans. Truman said, 'US foreign policy must be directed towards supporting free countries who resist attempts of subjugation by armed minorities or through external pressure'. This was the Truman Doctrine. Later Truman wrote that this was the turning point in American foreign policy and marked the beginning of American resistance to communist expansion in Europe and the Middle East.

The first countries to profit from American aid were Greece and Turkey. Greece received $250 million in military support and Turkey $150 million. Civilian and military advisors were sent to Greece to assist in the guerrilla war against a communist take-over. This war had become more tenacious since British troops had left Greece and the local communists were receiving support from neighbouring communist countries, particularly Bulgaria.

Jet fighters to Germany

In the spring of 1946 around 300 P-80 Shooting Stars were operational with the USAAF. The majority were stationed in the US but, according to USAF historian Robert T. Cossaboom Jr, a few of these jet fighters were based in Germany. The War Department allocated thirty-two P-80 jets to USAFE. The partially dismantled aircraft were shipped to Bremershaven, loaded on barges and floated up the Weser river to Bremen, and assembled by the 30th Mobile Repair Squadron. USAFE assigned the P-80s to the 31st Fighter Group at Giebelstadt. Later the P-80s were transferred to Kitzingen.

One major problem was that western European climate corroded the sensitive General Motors' turbojet engine which consequently had to be replaced frequently. In addition, a number of P-80s crashed during the European evaluation flights — the P-80's loss figures were the highest in the USAAF. Between March and September 1946 alone 36 aircraft were lost. No doubt

North American AT-6 Harvards were flown to Greece by USAFE pilots. *(MAP)*

As early as July 1947, the Greek air force, the Elliniki Aeroporia, received large numbers of North American AT-6 Texans which were flown to Greece by USAFE pilots. The AT-6 was really an advanced trainer but it could be armed. The Greek Texans were used against the communist guerrillas with reasonable success. The Greek air force were also given Douglas C-47s for troop transport and the rest of the dollar aid went on armoured vehicles, weapons, munitions and improvements to the military infrastructure, such as radar.

A unique strategic location

For financial reasons the British government was forced to leave the modernization of the Turkish military force to the US. As early as August 1946, the US had sharply criticised the Soviets' claim to the Dardanelles. When part of the US fleet steamed towards the eastern Mediterranean, General Eisenhower declared without any compromise that 'the Russians would not take a step that would irrevocably lead to a war'. With this he made it clear to the Russians that the Americans were not afraid of a hard confrontation over the Dardanelles.

Within the framework of the Truman Doctrine the US sent military advisors to supervise the modernization of the Turkish military force. The US also established several support posts that were used by the US Army and the USAFE for exercises. Several Turkish airfields, including the remote Incirlik air base south of Adana on the Gulf of Iskenderun, were proposed for permanent use by USAF units. This use would not be for 'peaceable' purpose only because Turkey, thanks to its

unique strategic location on the Black Sea and bordering on the Soviet Republics of Armenia and Gruziya, could count on a lot of interest from the American information services. Incirlik isolated by its surrounding swamps, was a regular departure point for American spy flights over the Soviet Union.

Problems in Berlin

Meanwhile, in Germany, tension over Berlin was rising. The fact that Berlin had not come completely under Soviet control after the war had always been a thorn in Russia's side. At Potsdam it had been decided that each of the Allies would occupy a sector of the city. The city was roughly divided into a Western occupation zone (America, Britain and later France as well) and an Eastern occupation zone (Russia). City administration remained a joint task for which an Allied Control Council was set up. The Commanders of all four Allies sat on the Council. Right from the first Council meeting the Russians pushed for each of the Western Allies to be responsible for provisions in their own sectors. It was also decided that all Council Decisions must be unanimous.

The problems arose after just a few meetings. The Russians wanted to keep to all the measures that they had taken before the establishment of the Allied Control Council and because the Russians had the power of veto all the measures taken by the Russians remained. Only when it was too late did the Western Allies see the grave mistake they had made. They had approved an administration in which the communists either ran or controlled the most important functions, such as monetary transfer, the police, the unions, the political parties and the press that exclusively spread communist propaganda. Obviously it was only a question of time before this would cause great problems.

Four Lockheed YP-80s were tested in Europe in 1945.
(Lockheed)

Even in the first months of the blockade the Russians allowed the American transport planes to pass unhindered through the corridors. They were, apparently, convinced that supplying two million civilians by air was an impossible task, even for the US Air Force. In this assumption Moscow made a big mistake; a mistake that in the end caused their blockade to fail.

Tigers to Fürstenfeldbruck

On the eve of the Berlin Airlift USAFE strength was low both in quantity and quality. With a total of just 458 aircraft of various types, there was not much left of the once-powerful USAFE. The Tactical Air Force comprised remaining elements of the European Air Transport Service (EATS) and the 9th Air Force.

The core was formed by two Troop Carrier Wings with Douglas C-47s and P-47s belonging to the 86th Fighter Bomber Group at Neubiburg air base near München. The USAFE's Tactical Air Force was obviously far too small to play a role of any significance if it actually came to an armed clash between East and West.

The CIA estimated there was a very real chance of an East-West confrontation and even predicted it. The Americans also feared the so-called domino effect. 'If Berlin falls, West Germany will follow,' was the expectation of American Military Governor General Clay. In July 1948 Washington transferred the 53rd Fighter Bomber Squadron (squadron name Tigers) — equipped with 75 Lockheed P-80B Shooting Stars from the canal zone to West Germany.

The 'Tigers' were the first squadron to be equipped with the Lockheed jet fighter, and along with two other squadrons formed the 36th Fighter Bomber Group at Fürstenfeldbruck air base. This move not only considerably increased the USAFE's fighting power, it was also of great psychological value in the Berlin conflict that by many was seen as one of the causes for the intensifying of the Cold War between East and West.

Experience from Indo-China

The Russians' mistake was inexplicable and appears to be simply a downright blunder. After all, it may be assumed that the military strategists in the Kremlin were aware of the apparent ease with which the American Air Transport Command maintained an extensive air bridge in Indo-China during World War 2. At the end of 1942 the American Air Force began provisioning its own army units in China from bases in India. American aid materials for the Chinese Chungking government were also transported via this air bridge which was everything except easy. First and foremost, the distances to be bridged were enormous. And the route went over the high Himalayan mountains. Despite these natural barriers 'the Hump', as the air bridge was called, was a great success and in every month 71,000 tons of food, fuel, munitions, etc, were flown to China.

General William H. Tunner, the man behind the Hump operation was brought to Europe to organize the Berlin Airlift.

Above: In 1948 Berlin was still one big ruin . . .
. . . and crowded by refugees. *(Landesbildstelle Berlin)*

Opposite: Every minute an aircraft . . . Douglas C-54 Skymaster approaching Tempelhof. *(Landesbildstelle Berlin)*

Operation 'Vittles'

In the early morning of 26 June 1948, two days after Moscow barred access to West Berlin, great activity prevailed at the American air base near Wiesbaden as lorries loaded with food, milk and medicines drove in and out. On the platform the valuable cargo was hand-loaded into waiting Douglas C-47 Gooney Bird transport aircraft. All around engines roared into life and heavily laden aircraft began trundling towards the runway. A long queue of C-47s quickly formed on the taxiway. Engines were warmed up and the last preflight checks were carried out until the take-off signal was given by the traffic controller.

With exasperating slowness the first C-47s stirred and took off sluggishly. Aircraft lifted into the air at intervals of a few minutes. their destination was Tempelhof airfield in the American sector of Berlin. Operation 'Vittles', the American code-name for the airlift, had begun. On the first day of Operation Vittles, 32 flights were made with Douglas Gooney Birds. In total nearly eighty tons of cargo were brought to the isolated city. Far too little, obviously, because the three Western sectors consumed 12,000 tons of fuel, food, clothing and medicine a day. Ferrying so much freight to Berlin every day would be almost impossible. It would take many hundreds of cargo aircraft.

The Berlin civilian population, placed total dependence on the airlift and it meant literally that their belts had to be tightened.

Allied co-operation

Royal Air Force Transport Command had also begun organizing an airlift to Berlin. The operation, first called 'Carter Paterson' and later renamed Operation 'Plainfare', was managed from the headquarters at Wunsdorf near Hanover. Operation Plainfare was carried out primarily with Douglas C-47 Dakotas and Avro York cargo aircraft. To reach Gatow airfield in the British sector of Berlin, the British used the short, central air corridor.

Co-operation between the two allies was both natural and necessary. Vittles and its British counterpart Plainfair were functionally combined into the Combined Air Lift Task Force (CALTF) with General Tunner in overall command. The absence of the French in the whole operation was noteworthy. To provision their sector in West Berlin the French had only three Junkers Ju 52 transports from a former Luftwaffe Transport-gruppe. For a while the French, who did not have an airfield at their disposal in their own occupation zone, operated from British Wunsdorf and flew to Gatow with their old aircraft.

But the French contribution to the airlift came to an early and sad end when two Junkers crashed into each other and were totally destroyed while taxiing at Wunsdorf. The French withdrew from the airlift; not a great deal could be done with just one airworthy old Junker.

Douglas C-47 Gooney Birds on Tempelhof. Despite the rain, food and other essentials are being unloaded after flight from Rhein Main or Wiesbaden. (US Air Force)

Bigger aircraft

The Americans had calculated that they could fly 4,500 tons of freight to Berlin per day. If they had to do it just with C-47s they would need 900. And that many C-47s were not available at that moment; many aircraft were sold off after the war or were in the Arizona desert waiting to be scrapped. Obviously, far fewer aircraft would be needed if larger aircraft could be used. Tunner's choice fell on the Douglas C-54 Skymaster; around 180 would be needed to transport 4,500 tons of freight per day. There were not that many to be found in Europe. In fact, it took Tunner until August 1948 to get just ten C-54s together in Wiesbaden.

The rest had to come from elsewhere. So the US Air Force's new transport organization, the Military Air Transport Service (MATS), was ordered to mobilize immediately all available C-54s and Fairchild C-82 Packets wherever they were in the world. Soon C-54s began arriving at Wiesbaden from America. Not only C-54s from the Air Force, because the American Overseas Airlines also made several of its DC-4s — the civil name of the C-54 — available for the airlift. The US Navy too heeded the call and sent two squadrons with a total of 21 R-5Ds — the marine version of the C-54 — from bases on Guam and Hawaii. With the influx of so many aircraft the airfield was soon over-full. The decision to use Rhein Main air base near Frankfurt as well was soon forthcoming and Celle and Fassberg airfields, used by the RAF, were also used by the Americans for Vittles.

Globemaster was too big

If larger aircraft were needed, why not turn straight to the world's biggest transport aircraft? The aircraft in question was the Douglas C-74 Globemaster of which the MATS had a number in service in the US. The dimensions of this four-engined aircraft were certainly massive for the time: length 38 metres, wingspan 53 metres and unladen weight of nearly 66 tons. This flying giant could transport around 25 tons over a distance of more than 3,300 kilometers. The maximum load weight was 33 tons!

On 11 August at Westover AFB, Massachusetts, a C-74 Globemaster from the MATS's 521st Air Transport Group prepared for a special mission to Germany. The C-74 would depart for Rhein Main within a few days with eighteen C-54 engines on board. On 17 August, after a flight via Lajes, the American support post on the Azores, the aircraft arrived at the West German air base. It was immediately 'commandeered' for Vittles and made 24 flights to Tempelhof and Gatow during the next few weeks, delivering 600 tons of freight to Berlin.

If Globemasters had been used wholesale, the scale of the airlift would have been much smaller. At least, far fewer flights would have been needed to bring the daily freight to Berlin. Tunner's calculation was that 68 C-74s could do the work of 180 C-54s moving the monthly 135,000 tons of freight in only 5,400 flights rather than the 13,800 needed with the C-54s. With a complete fleet of Globemasters, a total of 240,000 tons of freight could be moved per month.

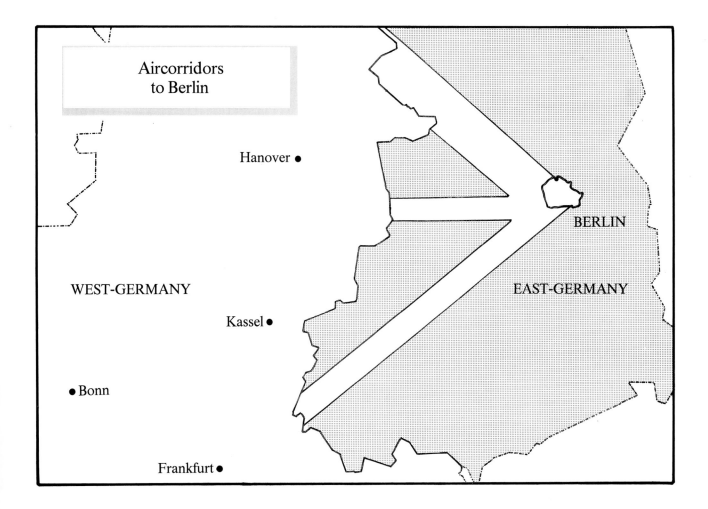

Douglas C-54 Skymasters on a misty morning on the flightline of Tempelhof. In the foreground a Douglas R-5D of the US Navy.
(*US Air Force*)

Unfortunately, the C-74 was too heavy for the Tempelhof and Gatow runways which were only provisional and consisted mainly of pierced steel planking — iron plates fixed to the stony under-layer with long pins to produce a runway. When these runways were laid, heavily laden C-54s just did not come into the calculations, which meant they had to be constantly repaired. At Tempelhof a team of 200 German workers were permanently at the ready with shovels and wheelbarrows full of sand and asphalt to quickly repair the damage after every landing.

An unladen Globemaster weighed twice as much as a C-54 full to the rim with coal. Multiple landings, in quick succession with heavily laden C-74s, would have completely destroyed the runways at Tempelhof.

Douglas C-74s were used under the code-name 'Goliath' for the regular transport of engines for the C-54 fleet in Germany. The engines were brought from the factory in the US to the 7540th Maintenance Group at Burtonwood in Lancashire, England, where the American C-54s were maintained and repaired.

General Tunner continued to try every alternative method available to deliver as much freight to Berlin per load as possible. One such method was to use converted Boeing B-29s carrying a large container in the bomb bay which made loading and unloading much faster.

★　　★　　★

SAC sends B-29s

Several weeks before the Russians blockaded Berlin, the Strategic Air Command, as a precautionary measure, sent a B-29 squadron from the 301st Bombardment Group to Fürstenfeldbruck air base and temporarily stationed two other squadrons from the 301st at Goose Bay air base, Newfoundland, Canada, where they were held in readiness for instant deployment to European bases. The American High Command hoped that the stationing of these atomic bombers would have a deterrent effect in the conflict. From Giebelstadt and Fürstenfeldbruck airfields, the heavy bombers could easily reach Moscow, a fact which the Kremlin would have to consider very seriously. On the other hand, the American strategists were aware of the safety risks posed by putting the B-29s so close to the Russian occupied zone — Giebelstadt and Fürstenfeldbruck were 100 and 200 kilometers from the Iron Curtain respectively and, therefore, well within the reach of Russian fighter-bombers operating from bases in East Germany and Czechoslovakia. All things considered, the SAC decided not to send future B-29 deployments to bases in Germany but to less vulnerable bases in England.

The first B-29s sent to England had already arrived by July 1948. They were from the 28th and 307th Bombardment Groups. All B-29 operations in England were placed under the command of the USAFE's newly formed 3rd Air Division, headquartered at the RAF Bomber Command base at Marham. According to the American historian Robert T. Cossaboom, the B-29s could operate from just about all the airfields the USAFE were using in England. Besides these, the RAF had put several other airfields at the Americans' disposal including Marham, Scampton and Waddington. Lakenheath, a large base in Suffolk, was also frequently used for B-29 operations. This base was even big enough to accommodate the giant Convair B-36 Peacemaker bombers. On 26 June 1948 the first of these intercontinental bombers were delivered to the SAC's 7th Bombardment Group at Carswell AFB, Texas. The Pentagon kept this strategic trump card up its sleeve for the time being.

★　　★　　★

Douglas C-54 shortly before touch-down at Tempelhof. *(US Air Force)*

Tunner averts a shambles

The use of different types of aircraft with different cruising speeds was a big headache for the American traffic controllers. The C-54 was much faster than the C-47 and to avoid overtaking them on the way, the C-54s always had to start first. Only when a group of C-54s was on the way could the C-47s start. As more aircraft began to take part in Vittles, the problems for General Tunner's Air Lift Task Force grew.

Vittles could easily turn into a complete shambles unless an efficient traffic system was introduced. This was made painfully clear to Tunner during one of his inspection flights. Commentator Robert Rodrigo wrote in his book *Berlin Airlift* that during this particular inspection flight in the autumn of 1948, Tunner was livid when, through a culmination of circumstances, two transport aircraft crashed one after the other at Tempelhof, completely blocking the two landing strips. Tunner's C-54 was 28th in a long queue of transport aircraft waiting to begin their approach.

Action was needed to prevent more accidents. General Tunner ordered all aircraft waiting to land at Tempelhof, back to their bases in West Germany. After this incident at Tempelhof a furious Tunner ordered that a new system for traffic control to and from Berlin be worked out and implemented.

'Baker Easy'

The special feature of the new traffic control system was the use of different flight altitudes. A vertical separation of 500 feet was introduced. This was sufficient separation to allow far more aircraft to use the air corridors at the same time. Moreover, under the new system the southern corridor was used exclusively for traffic from Wiesbaden and Rhein Main to Berlin. The northern corridor carried traffic from Celle and Fassberg and the increasing amount of RAF traffic. The central corridor was only used by traffic returning to the American bases in West Germany. These measures increased safety in the air considerably and that was Tunner's aim.

Henceforth, transport aircraft took off from one of the four American airfields at intervals of at least three minutes. A flight could, for example, start at Rhein Main where flying continued around the clock seven days a week. The pilot of any given C-54 called the tower shortly before take off and told the traffic controller that he wanted to make a 'Baker Easy' flight: 'Baker' meant the Rhein Main base and 'Easy' meant the C-54 wanted to go east — 'Easy' was destination Berlin. The traffic controller gave the exact flying altitude for the flight through the corridor and the time at which the aircraft must pass the Fulda radio beacon. Fulda lay exactly in the middle of the entrance to the southernmost corridor and formed an ideal starting point.

After take-off the aircraft climbed to 1000 feet and then turned southwards towards Darmstadt. Once above the Darmstadt radio beacon course was set for Aschaffenburg and from there final course change

69

The US Strategic Air Command was still using the ageing Boeing B-29s and B-50s. The picture shows a B-50 of the SAC 15th Air Force. *(US Air Force)*

America goes into top gear

Now it was known that the Soviet Union also had the atom bomb, American strategy had to be changed drastically. When their plans were first drawn up, the military planners in the Pentagon thought they still had plenty of time. Suddenly they had to change gear. Targets originally set for 1954 had to be reached by 1952.

The changes radically affected Strategic Air Command. SAC's nuclear force was still based on obsolescent B-29 and B-50 Superfortresses. These bombers had to be replaced by modern medium-sized jet-bombers such as the North American B-45 Tornado and the Boeing B-47 Stratojet. Meanwhile the massive Convair B-36 Peacemaker was introduced to the intercontinental force.

The Americans were well and truly anxious. On 15 December 1950, while the US Army, after six months of entanglement in the Korean War was under extreme pressure from the communist North Korean army, President Truman declared a state of national emergency. He was firmly convinced that the Western world could only stand if the communist threat was forestalled in Europe as well as in Asia. Almost as a matter of course the American President raised the defense budget to an unknown high; from $13 billion in the fiscal year 1949-50 to nearly $50 billion in the fiscal year 1952-53. This drastic increase was needed to finance the air force and army's new and ambitious plans.

According to these plans, revealed by the National Security Council in December 1950, by the end of 1952 the army was to comprise 24 divisions, while the air force by the same time should have grown to at least 94 Wings. To achieve this in such a short time the tempo of aircraft production was increased five-fold.

Demobilization had reduced the strength of the USAFE to an absolute low. At the end of the Berlin blockade, the 3rd Air Division, formed in 1948 to command B-29 operations in England, was quickly designated a Major Command and placed directly under USAF orders. Thus, of the USAFE organization little more remained than a single air division: the 2nd AD, which was headquartered at Landsberg air base just west of München. The USAFE's total fleet comprised 366 aircraft distributed over eight airfields, seven in Germany (Neubiburg, Fürstenfeldbruck, Rhein Main, Wiesbaden, Landsberg, Giebelstadt and Tempelhof) and one in Austria (Tulln, near Vienna).

For the USAFE the turn-around meant large scale modernization of the arsenal and a number of additional tactical fighting units. The first fighter units to be modernized were the 36th and 86th Fighter Bomber Wings which received a total of 180 Republic F-84E Thunderjets in place of their Lockheed Shooting Stars and Republic Thunderbolts. For the first time jet fighters were flown across the Atlantic *en masse* by the 27th Fighter Escort Wing (FEW) which was formed for this express purpose at Bergstrom AFB, Texas. The 27th FEW's pilots flew the F-84s, in two groups of 89 and 91 aircraft respectively, non-stop to Fürstenfeldbruck and Neubiburg. The crossings took place on 15 September (36th FBW) and 28 September 1950 (86th FBW). The over 9,000-kilometer crossing was made in thirteen hours without any stop-overs. On the way the Thunderjets were refuelled several times by KB-29Ps converted to flying fuel stations for the purpose.

American bases in the French Zone

Towards the end of 1950 the USAFE commanded two Tactical Wings, both equipped with modern F-84E fighters plus two Troop Carrier Groups stationed in Germany. A year later there were already seven Tactical Wings and, according to the plan, by the end of

Lockheed T-33 Shooting Star jet trainers were supplied to western airforces under the American military aid programme. Here a T-33A that the Italian Air Force received from the US in the early Fifties. *(Aeronautica Militare)*

1952, this was to have increased to eleven by which time the USAFE would command more than 1,000 aircraft. This large number of aircraft would obviously require more airfields. These were found primarily in England and France.

In February 1951, the US and France signed an agreement concerning the establishment of a large USAFE depot at Chateauroux air base south of Orléans in central France. The Americans desperately needed this depot as a staging station for the MDAP material that was being made available to the NATO partners in ever greater quantities. Chateauroux also became the logistics centre for the USAFE.

Further negotiations between Washington and Paris resulted in an agreement under which the Americans' use of the Chaumont-Semoutiers, Laon-Couvron and Toul-Rosières airfields was regulated. These three airfields lay in eastern France not far from the French occupation zone in Germany. From an 'Indiquant les terrains d'operations métropoles' of 1951 in which the French Ministry of Defense summarized all operational airfields in France, it appears that the US was allowed to use nine fields in France including Etain-Rouvres, Dreux-Semonches, Evreux-Fauville and Phalsbourg-Bourscheid. All these fairly extensive bases were used intensively by the USAFE throughout the 1950s.

The French also made several air bases in their German occupation zone available to the USAFE. In this case it was new air bases that still had to be constructed. The largest was built near the towns of Landstuhl and Ramstein on a site where during World War 2 first the Luftwaffe and later the USAAF had

used long stretches of a wide motorway as an emergency airfield. This new base actually consisted of two sections: one south of the motorway (Landstuhl) and one north of the motorway (Ramstein). Later, the road was completely diverted and both sections were brought together as one airfield. In the French occupation zone the newly built Bitburg, Spangdahlem (Binsfeld), Sembach and Hahn airfields were also handed over to the Americans.

In this way the US managed to put a large number of airfields at the disposal of the USAFE where the many new fighter units and the hundreds of extra jet fighters could be stationed.

Reconnaissance aircraft take the rap

On the other side of the Iron Curtain too, fast jet fighters were going into service. The new MiG-15 fighter (with the NATO name Fagot) became the Red Air Force's standard fighter and was primarily used as an interceptor. Western air forces feared the MiG patrols along the Eastern Bloc borders because the Russian pilots — often without any prior warning — opened fire immediately on aircraft that, perhaps through a navigational error, had wandered into Russian-occupied airspace, but also because Western aircraft that came too close to Russian fighters were fired upon without any apology.

President Truman, seen here inspecting a B-36A at Andrews Air Force Base in 1949, dramatically raised the American defense budget. *(US Air Force)*

The Russians considered the Western air violations a legitimate reason for immediate retaliatory attack. During the 1950s there were many such incidents which resulted in tens of aircraft being shot down or damaged by action. The Western air forces, especially the RAF and USAF, were not completely blameless. They regularly used the air corridors to Berlin as cover for spy flights over Soviet territory and American and British transport planes flew 'accidentally' out of the corridor on many occasions. The Russians were well aware that these aircraft were reconnaissance aircraft on espionage missions for the military intelligence services.

Little wonder then that the Russian pilots saw a potential sky spy that must be repelled with force or, worse, destroyed, in every aircraft that for whatever reason flew close to or over Soviet territory. Aviation journalist Dick van der Aart wrote in his book *Aerial Espionage* that even innocent Swedish, French and Belgian transport aircraft from civil airlines had to pay the price.

According to the official American summary of all air incidents between the US and Russia — not released for publication until 1984 — the first incident of an American aircraft being shot down by Russian fighters occurred on 8 April 1950. The aircraft was a US Navy Consolidated PB4Y-2 Privateer that had taken off in the morning from Wiesbaden Air Base. The Privateer, the marine version of the World War 2 B-24 Liberator, was flying over the Baltic near the large Russian Navy Base at Libau. According to the American statement, the aircraft was conducting electronic surveillance — a description frequently used for, for example, eavesdropping on military radio traffic. It is still not clear exactly where the spying Privateer was when it was fired on by MiG fighters and went down in the sea. The ten-man crew could not, in any event, relate their adventure.

On 8 October 1952 there was another confrontation. This time MiG-15 Fagots opened fire on a Douglas C-47 that was in the southernmost air corridor en route for Berlin's Tempelhof airfield. The C-47 was a so-called MEDEVAC version (Medical Evacuation) used for evacuating patients from West Berlin to Frankfurt. By heading for cover in the clouds at great speed the pilot narrowly escaped the attack.

A year and a half later, on 12 May 1954, two US Navy aircraft were the victims. The aircraft, probably AJ2P Savage reconnaissance aircraft, took off from a carrier in the Mediterranean for a mysterious flight along the Czechoslovakian border. Maybe it was a navigational error that caused the aircraft to go off course and enter Czech air space. Czechoslovakian air defense reacted by promptly sending several MiG-15s to intercept the intruders. The MiGs attacked without warning. The American intruders, although severely damaged, managed to get away and landed safely a short time later at the American air base at Neubiburg in Germany. The following day, Czech radio announced that two American aircraft had entered Czech airspace west of Domazlice and flown all the way to the uranium production centre near Jachymov. Hard proof has never been supplied. What exactly the two marine reconnaissance aircraft were doing in Czechoslovakia may forever remain a riddle.

MiGs attack Thunderjets

An air incident that roused the Cold War to its full intensity took place on 10 March 1953 over the American sector of Germany between Regensburg and the Czechoslovakian border. That afternoon, two Republic F-84E Thunderjet fighters from the 36th Fighter Bomber Wing at Fürstenfeldbruck air base took off on a routine patrol flight along the Czechoslovakian border. Once in the air the F-84s set a northerly course for Regensburg where they curved off in a southerly direction and flew parallel to the border.

Around two in the afternoon the F-84s were approaching Bayrischer Wald nature reserve flying at a height of 4,000 meters. Somewhere north of the villages of Regen and Zwiesel, Lieutenant Pilot Warren G. Brown called the attention of his wingman, Lieutenant Pilot Donald C Smith, to two MiG-15 fighters that were approaching at high speed from the direction of Czechoslovakia. The two Czech fighters kept a reasonable distance away from the surprised Americans and manoeuvred themselves behind them. Suddenly they opened fire with their cannon and Brown felt a severe jolt, his aircraft was badly hit. Smith, in the other F-84, managed to escape and returned with all haste to Fürstenfeldbruck.

Brown, whose aircraft was out of control and spinning towards the ground, was able to use his ejection seat and he came down in the farming hamlet of Einödhofes Hundessen. His aircraft crashed in flames at nearby Falkenstein close to the Czechoslovakian border. Strong US protest was not long in coming after the grave air incident. James Bryant Conant, senior American diplomat in Germany, called the bringing down of the F-84 over the American zone of Germany the worst piece of unpleasantness since the beginning of the Cold War between East and West.

Republic F-84E Thunderjets of the 36th Fighter Bomber Wing on the flightline at Bergstrom Air Force Base, Texas. The F-84Es made their Atlantic hop to Fürstenfeldbruck on 15 September, 1950.
(US Air Force)

The following day, George Wadworth, the US Ambassador in Prague, delivered a sharp letter of protest to the Czech authorities. The seriousness with which the Americans viewed the matter was shown by the fact that the letter was signed personally by John Foster Dulles, the American Secretary for Foreign Affairs. The US called the shooting down of the jet fighter over West German territory flagrant proof of the Eastern Bloc's aggressive attitude and considered the action a direct act of war — the MiGs were, indeed, many kilometres inside the American zone.

The American protest was, as expected, followed by fierce reaction from the Czechs. They took a strong stance against the American condemnation and, in their turn, accused the US of violating Czech airspace. According to a report in the *Nord Bayerische Nachrichten* several days after the shooting, the Czechs wanted to appear to believe that the two American F-84s were flying forty kilometers over the border across Czech territory and that Czech air defense wanted to force the aircraft to land. When this failed, the Czech pilots opened fire and, according to the Czech version, one F-84 managed to escape the interception while the other burst into flames and came down just over the border in West Germany. The American State Department ridiculed this explanation, calling it a complete fabrication.

Whatever possessed the Russians?

The story from Prague was so unbelievable that in diplomatic circles it was even speculated that the entire incident had been set up by the Soviets. The real question was, what had the Russians intended with the shooting? Was their anger meant as a warning to the Americans not to patrol too close to the Eastern Bloc border? Virtual proof of the correctness of this theory was supplied by the Russians themselves two days after the incident in Bavaria when they provoked a series of air incidents in an extremely aggressive way.

On 12 March 1953, Russian MiG-15s instigated an incident near Kassel in the American zone by carrying out a mock attack on a British aircraft. On the same day, Russian fighters even fired warning shots at a British commercial airliner that had wandered off course while in the southern air corridor en route for Berlin. And later in the afternoon, Russian aggressiveness reached a peak when MiG fighters shot down a Royal Air Force Avro Lincoln training bomber, killing six of the seven crew.

The Russian communiqué stated that the Lincoln had penetrated 120 kilometers into East Germany. On sighting the British aircraft the Russian High Command alerted MiG fighters for an intercept sortie. According to the Russians it was the British who opened fire on the fighters which retaliated immediately. Winston Churchill, the British Prime Minister, reacted furiously. First and foremost he refuted the Russian version of the incident because the four-engined Lincoln was unarmed. It was on a training flight in the northernmost air corridor and had veered off course due to a navigational error. At the time of the interception the aircraft was actually correcting the mistake and coming back to the air corridor. The Lincoln, which the Russians had fired on more than once, came down well inside the British zone and could, therefore, so went the British statement, at no time have penetrated 120 kilometers into East Germany.

With their abnormally harsh performance the Russians risked an international crisis of a severity as yet unknown in the Cold War. American reaction to the malicious shooting down of the F-84 was uncommonly fierce and even went so far as to talk openly of retaliation. 'I am convinced that the US knows what it has to do', James Bryant Conant told the German press.

Clearly the Americans could not leave the matter there. Measures would have to be taken. Thus, the American Supreme Command decided to replace the F-84E immediately with the North American F-86 Sabre interceptor fighter. The US Air Force had a great deal of faith in this new fighter — during the Korean War F-86 pilots brought down hundreds of MiG-15s. The F-86, a highly manoeuvrable air-superiority fighter with a top speed of 1,000 km/h was to redress the balance in Europe. On 19 March 1953 the 36th Fighter Bombardment Wing's first Sabres landed at Fürstenfeldbruck air base. Along with the new fighters the pilots received the order to shoot back if they were

Above: The American pilots received the order to shoot back when they were attacked. This propaganda photograph of airmen arming the cannons of a F-86 supported the Pentagon's strong language. *(DoD)*

Opposite: Three North American F-86A interceptors of the 81st Fighter Interceptor Wing take-off from Shepherd's Grove, England. The first F-86A Sabres of the USAFE were from the 116th Fighter Interceptor Squadron, a former Air National Guard unit that was called to active duty in February 1951. The 116th became part of the 81st Fighter Interceptor Wing based at Moses Lake Air Force Base, Washington. In August 1951 the 116th FIS moved to Shepherd's Grove, Suffolk, where the Sabres were deployed to bolster NATO. The 91st and 92nd FISs arrived a month later at Shepherd's Grove. *(US Air Force)*

attacked by Eastern Bloc fighters. The Americans could not have been more clear: the chips were down.

★   ★   ★

A transparent statement

Incidents between Russian and American aircraft also occurred regularly in southern Europe. But, perhaps because here the Americans were guilty of air violations, strong American protest was rarely forthcoming and any problems were solved behind the diplomatic screens. So the US was in a difficult predicament when on 27 June 1958 a Douglas C-118 Liftmaster was shot down over the Soviet Union.

The C-118 took off from Nicosia, Cyprus, with a cargo of freight for Tehran, Iran. In a severe storm over eastern Turkey the C-118 went off course and accidentally flew over Soviet Armenia. All this is according to the official American statement. But the Pentagon's story that the aircraft was an innocent transport was extremely thin. The C-118 was from the 7405th Combat Support Squadron at Wiesbaden air base in Germany. This mysterious squadron had several extraordinary Boeing EC-97G Stratofreighters at its disposal that were generally used for ELINT (Electronic Intelligence) missions along the Eastern Bloc borders. During these spy flights the EC-97s always carried ten or so Russian-speaking agents who listened-in on Russian radio frequencies.

A Lockheed C-130A-II Hercules of the mysterious 7406th
Operations Squadron photographed at Rhein Main, Germany. In
September 1958 a Hercules of this type was shot down over Armenia,
Soviet Union. *(MAP)*

The C-118 concerned in the incident was carrying a
crew of nine. The entire crew survived the crash and
was released by the Russians some time later. A normal
C-118 on transport duty only carried a maximum of
four crew members.

The next clash over Armenia came less than three
months later. This time it was an off-course Lockheed
C-130A-II Hercules that was shot down by Russian
fighters. And this time the aircraft was from the equally
mysterious 7406th Combat Support Squadron based at
Rhein Main. The aircraft departed Incirlik air base,
Turkey, on 2 September 1958 for a mission over eastern
Turkey. According to the offical statement the aircraft
was on a COMINT (Communications Intelligence)
mission which meant an eavesdropping flight along the
Russian border. Six of the seventeen crew were killed
in the incident. Their bodies were later returned to the
US by the Russians. But what happened to the
remaining eleven eavesdropping specialists is to this
day a riddle.

The final air incident of the 1950s occurred over the
Baltic on 7 November 1958. A SAC RB-47H Stratojet
belonging to the 55th Strategic Reconnaissance Squadron
based at Brize Norton in England was followed and
fired upon by Soviet fighters, although it was not, in
fact, hit by the Russian bullets.

★   ★   ★

Tornados in England

The Soviet Union's enormous conventional force posed
another problem for Washington for, whereas the
Russians had maintained personnel levels since the end
of World War 2, most of the US forces had been
demobilized. Russia was still, in fact, at war with
Germany and that was the excuse for maintaining the
Red Army at war strength.

The US sought an answer to Russian conventional
superiority in the expansion of their tactical nuclear
force, for example, by introducing more North American
B-45 Tornado jet-bombers.

Since the end of the 1940s Strategic Air Command
had had around a hundred of these four-engined jet
bombers, each capable of dropping five fairly small,
2,000 kg, tactical nuclear bombs. In the summer of
1952 the American Supreme Command in Washington
decided to station B-45s in England. Three squadrons
that formed part of the newly established 47th Bombardment Wing stationed at Sculthorpe air base, Norfolk,
were deployed at the same time. The three squadrons
of the 20th Fighter Bomber Wing based at Wethersfield
air base in Essex were equipped with Republic F-84G
Thunderjets. These jet fighters, which were specially
converted to carry small atomic bombs, came from San
Antonio AFB in Texas and, like the B-45s, flew to their
English base via Greenland and Iceland.

The bomber gap

The Soviet Union was also not standing still. On 8
August 1953 Georgi Malenkov, Chairman of the

Council of Ministers of the Supreme Soviet, brought all adherents of the East/West *détente* out in a cold sweat. He announced that the Soviet Union had, for some time, had the H-bomb. This news dropped on the Americans almost literally like a bomb. The H-bomb was a new nuclear weapon with a destructive power many times greater than the original atom bomb. The H-bomb used the high temperature released by an atom splitting to set nuclear fusion in motion. Russian nuclear experts had mastered this complicated process ahead of the Americans. They had also succeeded in conducting a test explosion with this new nuclear bomb somewhere in Siberia at the beginning of August. This gave the Russians about a three-month lead in the arms race. The Americans did not test a hydrogen bomb until 16 November, on the Marshall Islands in the Pacific Ocean.

It is remarkable that the Americans could not register the powerful Russian explosion in Siberia. It is all the more astonishing because the Air Force Applications Center was conducting intensive nuclear research in the atmosphere with converted B-29s and B-50s. One plausible explanation may be that the many above-ground atomic tests had released so much radioactive dust into the atmosphere that reliable measuring was no longer possible.

According to Western intelligence agencies, the Soviets had already begun development of a series of long-range bombers to carry the new H-bomb in 1952. These were the Tupolev Tu-16 (NATO code-name Badger) with a range of between 5,700 and 7,800 kilometers, the Tu-95 (NATO code-name Bear) with an extreme range of between 12,500 and 17,500 kilo-

Patrolling F-84Es of the 36th Fighter Bomber Wing along the German and Czechoslovakian borders were relentlessly attacked by Eastern Bloc fighters. *(US Air Force)*

meters depending on the version, and the Myasishchyev M-4 (NATO code-name Bison) with a range of between 10,000 and 12,000 kilometers. Western observers were amazed when on 1 May 1954 both the Tu-16 Badger and the M-4 Bison took part in the famous May Day parade over Moscow's Red Square.

Bill Gunston, the authoritative British aviation journalist, wrote in his book *Aircraft of the Soviet Union* that the Tu-95 Bear flew just four months later and almost immediately went into mass production. In May 1955 — less than a year after the first flight with a Tu-95 — Western diplomats attending an air show at Tuschino AB near Moscow saw a large number of Bears fly past.

These developments were used by the 'hawks' in the American Congress to persuade public opinion that in the weapons field the Russians had left the US behind. In February 1956, Democrat Senator Henry Jackson compared the development time of the Bison bomber and the B-52 — the bomber SAC intended as successor to the B-36 intercontinental bomber. The Soviets planned to produce 25 Bisons per month while the US could only build twelve B-52s per month. Jackson foresaw the 'Bomber Gap' that threatened to develop between the US and the Soviet Union if production of the American bomber was not drastically increased.

A short while later, General Curtis LeMay, Commander of the USAF, predicted that the Soviet Union's strategic air force would overtake that of the US in 1959. This, according to him, could put the US in grave danger.

Above: The Tupolev Tu-16 Badger was one of the Soviet Union's new bombers to which America had to find an answer. The Badger was first noticed by Western observers during the military parade in Moscow on 1 May 1954. *(MAP)*

Top: The Boeing B-47 Stratojet was with a maximum speed of over 1000 km/h the world's fastest bomber. *(Boeing)*

LeMay and Jackson were both supporters of a hard line against the Soviet Union, which they did not trust. They were also fierce opponents of communism and with their Bomber Gap theory they played cleverly on the American citizen's fear of communism. Their action produced results because B-52 production was drastically increased and eventually 744 were built.

The nuclear deterrent

With three squadrons of B-45s and three squadrons of F-84Gs stationed in England, the USAFE had a tactical nuclear offensive force at their disposal. This posting must be seen as compensation for the fact that NATO commanded far fewer conventional forces. According to the 'Rapport Palme', the final report of the Independent Commission for Disarmament and Security Questions led by the Swede Olaf Palme, published in 1982, the policy adopted with this move put the emphasis on fast or, if necessary, first use of nuclear weapons.

Stationing the bombers at British air bases, from where parts of the Soviet Union were within range, offered a certain amount of support to America's strategic plans. The B-45s and F-84s were, nevertheless, tactical weapons systems. They were elements of the USAFE organization and were deployed as part of NATO's Tactical Nuclear Capability. Their prime task was the support of ground troops in central Europe.

The Pentagon's strategy was, however, based on massive retaliation against Russia if the Soviet Union started a war. This plan, code-named 'Trojan', meant Strategic Air Command going into full scale action. Trojan's 'backbone' was formed by the Boeing B-47A Stratojets that had been in service with SAC since the end of 1951. The Stratojet could reach a speed of more than 1,000 km/h, which at the time was faster than most interceptor fighters, and fly for 7,000 kilometers without refuelling — more than enough to be able to strike at large tracts of the Soviet Union from bases in Alaska and Western Europe.

To support the Trojan strategy the 7th Air Division was established in May 1951. The 7th used many of the 3rd Air Division's bases in England. Reconstruction of four former RAF bases was also begun. Work to make these airfields — Fairford, Brize Norton, Upper Heyford and Greenham Common — suitable for use by B-47s included lengthening the take-off and landing strips and building concrete bunkers for the nuclear weapons.

In the summer of 1953 the 7th Air Division began a system of B-47 temporary deployments to English bases. These temporary duty postings (TDY) generally involved an entire Wing of 45 B-47s, together with around twenty Boeing KC-97 Stratofreighters (flying tankers), being held at readiness at an English base for ninety days. At the end of the TDY period they were relieved by another Wing that was, generally, stationed at a different airfield. These temporary postings soon became a heavy burden for both the SAC organization and Military Air Transport Service which had to transport thousands of personnel and tons of material to and from the US in just a few days every time the B-47s rotated.

More importantly, the B-47s began to suffer noticeably from the intensive use. In 1958 it was decided the TDY postings would be replaced by a new system of overseas deployments called Reflex. Reflex was tested in July 1958 at Sidi Slimane air base, Morocco. From then on, rather than a complete Wing of 45 B-47s being stationed for ninety days only, twenty B-47s from four Wings were stationed in England at any given time. During their three-week Reflex deployment each aircraft was on full alert for instant take-off with a full nuclear load for exactly one week.

Within fifteen minutes

The introduction of the Reflex deployments was also intended to support a new strategic concept based on one third of SAC's fleet being able to get into the air within fifteen minutes. For this 'Quick Reaction Alert' to be possible more Reflex deployment bases were needed. In July 1958 — at the same time as Reflex was introduced — SAC established the 16th Air Force at Torrejon air base in Spain. According to a bi-lateral agreement between the US and Spain, the American air force could henceforth use not only Torrejon air base near Madrid but also Zaragoza, Moron and Rota air bases.

Eleven North American B-45A Tornado bombers of the 47th Tactical Bomber Wing lined-up at Goose Bay Air Base, Canada. The B-45s were deployed to Sculthorpe Air Base in 1952.
(Smithsonian Institution)

Although the B-47s were fitted with powerful turbojet engines they were later also equipped with disposable (auxiliary) rocket engines that provided additional thrust during take-off. This Jet Assisted Take-Off (JATO) enabled the B-47 to climb to its operating height far more quickly.

In practice, spectacular JATO starts were rarely made. As few, in fact, as genuine 'alert scrambles'. During the full-alert phase of the deployment a (practice) alarm was sounded almost daily upon which the crew sprinted to their bombers and engines were hastily started. Many times they then taxied at high speed to the runway from where they returned to the dispersal point. Only seldom did the B-47s make an actual alert scramble.

These exercises were a daily routine at most of the SAC bases throughout the world. No simple exercise let it be said, the less so if one considers that at the end of 1958 SAC had a strategic fleet of over 3,200 aircraft; 1,396 B-47 Stratojets with 745 KC-97 Stratofreighters and 488 B-52 Stratofortresses with 322 fast Boeing KC-135 Stratotankers. The 'fifteen-minute' concept meant that 24 hours a day every day one thousand aircraft were in a state of readiness.

The North American B-45A Tornado bombers of the 47th Tactical Bomber Wing were used to carry out NATO's Tactical Nuclear Capability. Here a B-45 is seen taking off from Sculthorpe. In the foreground two Boeing KB-29 tankers. *(US Air Force)*

The French connection

In the middle of the 1950s, when the Cold War was at its hottest, substantial disagreement arose within the Western Alliance concerning West Germany's future. This country's rearmament severely tested the relationship between the US and France.

In 1951, in Paris, the Ministers of Foreign Affairs of France, Italy, West Germany, the Netherlands, Belgium and Luxembourg signed an accord for the establishment of a European Community for Coal and Steel (ECCS). The fundamental principle behind the establishment of the ECCS was to make a new war impossible. By giving a supra-national organization control of the basic materials needed by the defense industry, the likelihood of revived rearmament (of Germany and Italy) was considerably limited. The Americans in particular saw a trend in this French initiative towards European integration. To them the time seemed ripe to put a proposal for West Germany's inclusion in NATO before the NATO Council. France was the only member state to disagree sharply with this American proposal.

It was the nationalistic Gaullists in the French government who were most violently opposed to the rearming of Germany. Agreement was reached concerning the Alliance's strategy of forward defense. If one wished to organize a defence against communist aggression, it was reasoned, then the aggressor's troops should be stopped as early as possible (in West Germany). Moreover, Europe had come to realise that it could only raise sufficient forces for its defense if every European country co-operated, including West Germany.

France was in a difficult position. First and foremost its Indo-China policy and the fight against the Viet Minh relied on support from the US. And the French economy was being reconstructed with considerable financial support from America. This had led to France becoming virtually a US dependent which meant it was obliged to submit a counter proposal. In October 1950 René Pléven the French Minister of National Defense submitted a plan for the creation of a European Army to the French Assembly. The Pléven Plan for a European Defense Alliance followed the same lines as the ECCS, i.e., integration under supra-national supervision. Two months later, during a meeting of the NATO Council in Brussels, it was decided that France would organize a conference of all the European countries that could possibly contribute to a European army.

The conference was held in February 1951 and led to the establishment of the EDA (European Defense Alliance). The treaty was signed by France, West Germany, Italy, and the Benelux countries on 27 May 1952. Ratification took a little longer. First France submitted a new proposal which increased its own role, but as it also affected the supra-national character of the EDA it was unacceptable to the other countries. It very soon appeared that the French-originated plan for a supra-national European Army would, carefully, be delayed by French resistance.

Charles de Gaulle, who had retired from active politics in 1946, was particularly busy behind the scenes stirring up strong opposition to the EDA treaty. During a press interview at the beginning of 1954 he said that he could guarantee that the EDA (and the rearming of Germany) would not go through. 'I will do anything to prevent it [the EDA treaty]. I will work with the Communists to block it,' he threatened. Le Général and his supporters within the French government did not want any supra-national body having authority over their own troops. Neither did de Gaulle want to co-operate in the rearmament of Germany and, to a lesser degree, Italy. On 30 August, after a two-day debate, the French Assembly voted against the EDA treaty: Europe was a vision the poorer.

France's failure, since they could not live with their own proposal, did, however, bring West Germany's participation in NATO, closer. On the initiative of

The bomber gap was finally filled with 744 big eight-jet Boeing B-52 Stratofortresses, the first entering service in 1955. The B-52 had an almost unlimited combat range, because it could be refuelled in-flight by either Boeing KC-97 Stratofreighters or Boeing KC-135 Stratotankers that entered the SAC service in 1957. *(US Air Force)*

Anthony Eden, the British Minister of Foreign Affairs, West Germany and Italy were invited to join the existing West European Union (WEU). The WEU Treaty was signed in Brussels in 1948 by Great Britain, France, the Netherlands, Belgium and Luxembourg. This treaty, also called the Brussels Pact, covered co-operation in the economic, social, cultural and military fields. As far as the last was concerned this involved collective self-defense and mutual military assistance. Eden's proposal was accompanied by a recommendation to the NATO Council that West Germany and Italy be nominated members of NATO.

Membership of the West European Union was discussed in October 1954 during a summit conference of the WEU countries in London. France could do no more than propose a few conditions. For example, the new WEU treaty should bar West Germany from manufacturing NBC weapons (nuclear, biological and chemical weapons) and limit West Germany's forces to a maximum of half a million personnel.

On 6 May 1955 the WEU treaty came into force and three days later West Germany and Italy became members of NATO

★   ★   ★

American reaction to the situation was as businesslike as it was surprising. Officially it was stated that the US considered the entire crisis a trade disagreement around the control of an international, monopolistic and public utility. In the eyes of the Americans, the Canal Company was an Egyptian Corporation and as such liable to Egyptian legislation. For the rest the US played down the entire affair seeing it, as the American Secretary for Defense Charles Wilson remarked at the time, as no more than a political ripple. In fact, Washington feared that the Suez Crisis would escalate directly into a global crisis. The Kremlin had already let it be known that they were prepared to step in on Egypt's side, a threat the US took seriously.

Peter Wright, a former official with MI5 — British counter-espionage — revealed in his book *Spycatcher* that by spying on the Egyptian Embassy in London the British had discovered reports of secret Egyptian/Russian talks from which it appeared that Moscow had planes ready to send — if necessary — against the British.

Israel guards the back door

America's attitude caused bad blood between the US and France which manifested itself among the French as a budding anti-Americanism that would later come to full bloom under de Gaulle.

England and France were prepared to defend their interests in the Middle East whatever the cost and were determined on a reckoning with Nasser. The military staff worked feverishly on a joint military plan and soon stumbled over several problems, one of the most difficult of which was air cover. Neither the French nor the British had suitable support installations in the area from where an air strike could be launched. Only Akrotiri airfield on Cyprus was suitable but it was really too far from the Egyptian targets and could only be used for operations with English Electric B-2 Canberra bombers. And for an attack from Libya, the agreement of the influential Americans was necessary.

For a successful air strike via the Sinai Desert, a friendly air force with sufficient air bases in the area was needed. Wanting to put an end to the continuous attacks from the Sinai Desert by Egyptian Fedayeen, the Israelis offered to help.

On 29 October Israeli troops crossed the Egyptian border and simultaneously approximately 400 Israeli paratroops dropped from French aircraft near the Mitla Pass 45 kilometers east of Suez. The French Air Force also provided air cover for the Israeli advance in the Sinai using, among others, Republic F-84F Thunderstreaks operating from bases in Israel. Meanwhile, British aircraft bombarded Egyptian airfields. So began a dangerous military operation that under pressure from the Security Council, and America, ended on 6 November 1956 with a cease-fire being declared.

Following the Hungarian Revolt in 1956, USAFE furnished extensive logistic support for operation 'Safe Haven'. Before the Soviet-backed Hungarian government closed the borders, nearly 200,000 refugees fled the country. In the period 11 December 1956 to 2 January 1957 the USAFE airlifted some 9700 Hungarian refugees to new homes in the US. Douglas C-124 Globemasters of the Military Air Transport Command were used to transport medical supplies to Vienna.
(US Air Force)

Above: All North American F-100 Super Sabres of the three USAFE fighter wings in France had to leave the country. *(MAP)*

Top: The Israeli offensive was supported by France which bombed Egyptian targets using Republic F-84F Thunderstreaks operated from bases in Israel. At the same time the British Royal Air Force bombed several others west of the Suez Canal.
(Service Historique de l'Armée de l'Air)

Peacemaker on the warpath

The Soviet Union made good use of the political situation of autumn 1956. While the US had its hands full with the British/French/Israeli actions against Egypt, Russia invaded Hungary to crush an uprising against the communist regime. On 24 October 1956 the uprising reached its peak when an estimated hundred thousand Hungarians demonstrated in Heroes Square in Budapest. Four days earlier American Defense Secretary Wilson had, as a precaution, ordered Strategic Air Command to deploy sixteen Convair B-36H Peacemaker long-range bombers to England. They landed on 21 October after a non-stop flight over the Atlantic. It was perchance the first time that such a large number of B-36s had been sent to an overseas USAF base; it was perhaps also the first time since the Berlin Crisis of 1948 that the US so openly threw its nuclear power into the political ring.

Exactly how long the B-36s' British deployment lasted is not known, neither is it known whether the B-36s were at nuclear alert during their stay and were ready to use the feared hydrogen bomb. Indications

were that the American Peacemakers were on the warpath, something that was supposed to shock the Kremlin. But the Soviets gave all the signs of not being in the least intimidated even by the mighty B-36s. In any event, the American show of force did not restrain them on 4 December 1956 when they made a bloody end to the Hungarian uprising. Thirteen days after the uprising Russian tanks literally ripped the hopes of the Hungarian people into shreds.

American reaction was not directly forthcoming. Not until two days later, on the day of the American presidential elections, did President Eisenhower proclaim a state of emergency for the American forces. From that moment SAC units all over the world were brought to the highest state of readiness. This included the 310th Bombardment Wing from Smokey Hill AFB in the US that was stationed at Greenham Common air base, England, as part of a Reflex TDY. The American Strategic Air Command bared its teeth and the Russians smiled.

De Gaulle shows the USAFE the door

Towards the end of the 1950s considerable rumblings were heard within the NATO Alliance. Once again it was France's attitude that caused the problems. And this time it was America's storage of atomic weapons on French territory that the French found indigestible. When Charles de Gaulle was elected President in December 1958, it was expected that he would do something about France's declining political role in Europe (and the Middle East and North Africa). De Gaulle's aim was the reinstatement of a French presence in world politics. France was not going to shelter under the American atomic umbrella because, de Gaulle was convinced, France could not maintain its influence as a major power without its own nuclear weapons. Within this framework France's own nuclear strike power 'Force de Frappe' supported the new, independent foreign policy that de Gaulle would brandish from now on.

De Gaulle was certainly no enthusiastic supporter of America's Euro-policy and did not hide his opinion of the role America had chosen to play in the Suez Crisis. Six months after his election he demanded the immediate removal of all the nuclear weapons the USAFE had stationed at bases in France. This involved the removal of a total of 180 supersonic North American F-100 Super Sabres from the 48th, 49th and 50th Tactical Fighter Wings that were stationed at Chaumont, Etain and Toul-Rosières air bases respectively.

The USAFE could do little else than obey de Gaulle's order, and began in July 1959 under the code-name 'Red Richard' with the relocation of the three fighter groups. The 49th and 50th TFWs were posted to Spangdahlem and Hahn air bases in German Eifel. The former SAC base at Lakenheath in England was made ready for the three squadrons of the 48th TFW. The Super Sabres of the 48th TFW left France on 15 January 1960.

Less than a month later the French held their first nuclear test at Reggane in the southern Sahara desert. France had taken its first step towards nuclear independence.

Chapter 6
The turbulent sixties

During the Cold War, the US put total trust in the 'Massive Response' defense strategy. According to this doctrine, for which the American National Defense Council had laid down guidelines in 1956, every communist activity, in particular a Soviet military attack aimed at Western Europe, would be answered with a massive nuclear retaliatory attack on Russian targets. The threat of massive nuclear reprisal had become a component of American politics and it was Republican President Dwight E. Eisenhower, Supreme Commander of the Allied forces during World War 2, and his Vice President Richard M. Nixon, who put 'nuclear diplomacy' into practice, openly using nuclear retaliation as a threat.

Such threats were generally made in passing, at press conferences, for example. This was the case in 1956, during both the Suez Crisis and the Russian invasion of Hungary, and in 1958, when Russian Party Leader

In the sixties, the USAFE air defenses were reinforced with the Convair F-102A Delta Dagger interceptor. *(Tonl van Schaik)*

Nikita Khrushchev aimed serious threats concerning the status of Berlin at the US.

The Massive Response tasks were in the hands of Strategic Air Command (SAC) which, since 1955, had had several hundred colossal eight-engined Boeing B-52 Stratofortress intercontinental bombers and more than 1,500 Boeing B-47 Stratojet medium/long-range bombers at their disposal for this purpose. In 1960 the Convair B-58 Hustler entered service with two wings. The B-58's large aerodynamic delta wing and four powerful General Electric J-79 jet engines, the same engines as in the Lockheed F-104 Starfighter and early models of the McDonnell Douglas F-4 phantom, provided a supersonic top speed and a high cruise altitude. The SAC also commanded several missile squadrons equipped with strategic missiles. These were Atlas and Titan Intercontinental Ballistic Missiles (ICBMs), with a range of over 5,000 kilometers, and Jupiter and Thor Intermediate Range Ballistic Missiles (IRBMs) with a range of 1,000 to 5,000 kilometers, a

good number of which were deployed in Europe along the border with the Iron Curtain.

The nuclear forces of both super powers were roughly equal. And it was, in fact, this balance that stopped the American Massive Response doctrine from working as a concept for nuclear deterrence.

We can at least assume that the opponent's answer to a wholesale nuclear attack would be immediate and devastating. An American attack would, therefore, lead directly to the destruction of the US and in this case Europe. In addition, the large number of tactical atomic weapons sited in Europe, hardly made the American nuclear deterrent a plausible proposition. These small atomic weapons were intended for a Limited Nuclear Response, ie, for a limited atomic war. This strategy was a perfect example of the minimal rationality in the American military's perception at that moment. Any use of these tactical weapons in a limited conflict would, irrevocably, lead to a worldwide catastrophe: indeed, the explosive power of most of these small atomic weapons, thousands of which were stockpiled in European depots, was many times greater than the power that wiped Hiroshima from the face of the earth. And the combined explosive power of the tactical atomic weapons deployed in Europe was thousands of times greater than the explosive power of all the bombs — including the two atom bombs — available to the Allies at the end of World War 2.

How great then was the frighteningly large explosive power of the large strategic atomic weapons? They were so enormous and the stockpiles of nuclear weapons in the US and the Soviet Union were so large that people had begun to talk of a senseless 'overkill'.

Nuclear policy fails

The wholesale retaliation doctrine had only a limited military value. Possibly it restrained the opponent from beginning a nuclear attack or making a conventional (non-nuclear) attack on Europe. But whether the doctrine could be used as a universal panacea was by no means certain. During the 1950s, at least, the greatest communist threat to the free world was not a nuclear attack but rather the non-nuclear methods the communists were using to try and achieve their goal. Intimidation, infiltration, insurrection and guerrilla

Mace cruise missiles from the 30th Tactical Missile Wing at Hahn Air Base, Germany, photographed in early 1963. *(DoD)*

A Jupiter Intermediate Range Ballistic Missile (IRBM) is put into position at the Italian missile base Cioiio del Colle in the spring of 1960. *(Dod)*

activities were the communists' main weapons and against these the American nuclear might was ineffective. And so the US's nuclear policy failed.

Primarily, it was John F. Kennedy who denounced this shortcoming. In his book about the life of Kennedy, Theodore C. Sorensen, one of Kennedy's close colleagues, wrote that this was why the Presidential candidate's election campaign included frequent references to the need for extending and modernizing the US's conventional forces. Kennedy stressed that it was impossible for a president to reach for an atomic weapon in every situation. He pointed out that communist aggression could also be combatted effectively by conventional means. Extending its conventional forces would boost the plausibility of American military diplomacy, theoretically, allowing the President to react to every situation with the most suitable weapons. The options would even include waging a limited conventional war, an impossibility with nuclear weapons.

As soon as he was elected US President in November 1960, Kennedy drew a heavy line through the massive response strategy and ordered his Defense Secretary, Robert McNamara, to give top priority to the introduction of a Flexible Response Strategy. By going straight to the ultimate means at his disposal Kennedy gave immediate power to his actions. Within the framework of the new strategy both the US Army and the US Air Force were drastically modernized. It goes without saying that this brought with it many changes in duties. One result of these changes was that the Air National Guard (ANG) became the hub of the conventional forces.

The ANG became a fast response force that could, at any given moment, be deployed as a conventional extension of the United States Air Force Europe (USAFE). And because the emphasis of the ANG now lay on tactical support, various interceptor squadrons previously under the Air Defense Command (ADC) were now placed organizationally under the Tactical Air Command (TAC).

With the advent of the new Flexible Response strategy, the USAFE hastened the introduction of the Convair F-102A Delta Dagger air defense fighter in a total of six interceptor squadrons. These six squadrons — two in Spain, three in Germany and one in the Netherlands — were units of the newly formed 86th Air

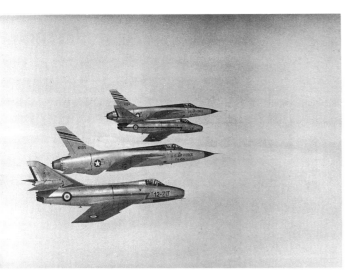

The 49th and 36th Tactical Fighter Wings from the USAFE at Spangdahlem and Bitburg were re-equipped with the Republic F-105D Thunderchief fighter bomber. Here two F-105Ds from the 36th TFW are seen in formation with two Mystère B2s from the French Air Force at Cambrai Air Base. *(DoD)*

Division, headquartered at Ramstein air base, and the 65th Air Division, headquartered at Torrejon, Spain.

In June 1961 the USAFE was also given command of three squadrons equipped with Republic F-105D Thunderchief fighter-bombers. At the time the F-105 Thunderchief was the USAF's heaviest and most advanced combat aircraft. The single-seater aircraft could carry a bomb load of more than seven tons; more than twice the load that could be carried by a World War 2 Boeing B-17 Fying Fortress! Moreover, because the F-105 was a so-called 'all-weather fighter', it could fly whatever the weather, which made its operation in Europe's changeable climate a good deal easier.

The modernization programmes and reorganizations were still in full swing when a new, turbulent world crisis developed. Once again Berlin was the stage. It was Kennedy's first chance to prove his Flexible Response doctrine was right.

The splinter in the heart of Europe

Berlin has always played a major role in American foreign policy and, since 1945, has determined to a great degree the political climate between East and West.

Nowhere in the world was the difference between communism and capitalism so visible as in Berlin. Nowhere were the two systems so close together. The presence of the Western Allies, in Soviet-controlled East Germany no less, stuck in the Kremlin's craw. The Soviet Union made many attempts to get the Western sector of Berlin under her control as well. The brutal blockade of 1948 was a bizarre climax to this political game. During the 1950s, after the annexation of West Berlin had failed, this already isolated sector of the city was gradually shut-off on the eastern side. The great value the US attached to the free status of West Berlin led to America pledging itself to protect three goals: first and foremost, the democratic right of the people of West Berlin to choose their own political system; second, the presence of Western troops for as long as this was desired by the residents; and third, unhindered access to the city from West Germany via transit routes

and air corridors through Soviet-controlled East Germany.

It was logical that in 1958 the White House dismissed a German peace treaty out of hand. A peace treaty — the heart's desire of communist party leader Khrushchev — would legitimize the partition of Germany and could put an end to the Allies' occupation rights within East Germany. Without a doubt, the subject of 'Berlin' would have been high on the agenda of the four superpowers' summit conference on 16 May 1960.

Eleven days previously a Lockheed U-2 on a spy flight from Incirlik, Turkey, over the Soviet Union had come down after being hit by a Russian air defense missile. For Khrushchev, the spy scandal was a direct pretext to boycott the summit meeting and stay away from Paris. Khrushchev had let it be known that a settlement for Berlin had to be agreed before April 1961. He announced, triumphantly, that he would 'remove this splinter' in the heart of Europe. This was threatening language from the Soviet leader, but his words quickly petered out because behind the diplomatic screens a meeting between him and President Kennedy was hastily arranged and took place in the first week of June.

The consultations in Vienna

Party leader Khrushchev and President Kennedy met on 3-4 June for two long consultations. Although the second day included an exhaustive exchange of ideas about Berlin, this did not lead to any results. During these discussions, Khrushchev continually harped on about the importance of a joint German peace treaty adding, as a direct link to this, that the Soviet Union would sign an independent peace treaty with East Germany if the Western Allies and the 'aggressive, revengeful West Germans', did not wish to work with them on a communal solution. With this peace treaty the state of martial law that still applied would cease and both the occupation rights and the Western Allies' rights to free access, including the use of the air corridors to Berlin, would be annulled.

President Kennedy answered that Berlin meant a great deal to the United States. He told Khrushchev that the world would no longer attach any value to American agreements if America accepted the loss of Berlin's rights, as this would mean the West Berliners had been left in the lurch by America. It would also be the end of any hope for the reunification of the two Germanies. Kennedy emphasized his determination to keep America's commitments to Berlin. The Russian leader got the message. He reacted violently, saying that if the United States were so keen to start a war over Berlin, then perhaps the Soviets had better sign the peace treaty immediately so that they could get on with it.

What the President really meant was that there was a substantial difference between the Soviets signing a peace treaty and the handing over of the West's rights to the East Germans. Encroachment of the West's rights was, in Kennedy's view, an act of war. Khrushchev stressed that once the peace treaty was signed, the Western Allies' presence in East Germany would be illegal and would be seen as an incursion of East Germany's borders which would be resisted:

force would be fought with force. The peace treaty, Khrushchev stated, would be signed in December and the United States had better begin its preparations as the Soviet Union would do so as well. Without the summit meeting in Vienna having achieved anything, the two leaders once again went their separate ways. No agreements had been made and the threats that had been bandied backwards and forwards only increased the risk of military action.

An enormous problem

Clarification of the American position was, really, the only achievement of the Vienna summit meeting. The West's rights in West Berlin were held on to with a firm grip and, according to Kennedy, were even worth a nuclear war with the Soviet Union.

There was one really enormous problem and that was the credibility of the American nuclear threat. If a peace treaty between the Soviet Union and East Germany was signed, the West's access routes could be blocked by a handful of East German army companies. And West Berlin, surrounded as it was by East German territory, could easily and very quickly be occupied by Soviet troops. The mainly American occupation troops in West Berlin would have very little effect and would be unable to prevent a blockade by Russian and East German forces. The Americans would be faced with two options; launch a nuclear attack at once or do nothing. The President could choose between wholesale destruction or humiliation.

Here, once again, it was clear that the massive response strategy was totally wrong for the defense of Western interests. The Western hemisphere had put its faith in this strategy for many years and felt protected under the American atomic bomb umbrella. Such was the faith in the nuclear retaliation strategy that large gaps had gradually been allowed to appear in NATO's conventional defenses. Now the day of reckoning had come. The atom bomb was all the West had and, naturally, the Soviets never believed that the President would gamble the existence of his own country merely to preserve a Western enclave in East Germany. The President obviously came to the same conclusion. He sought, therefore, for ways to fill the defense/credibility

The roads to and the western part of Berlin could be easily blocked by the Soviet forces. *(Landesbildstelle Berlin)*

gap on a scale that would also be convincing to the Kremlin. Kennedy's answer was a military force large enough to prevent East German troops from occupying West Berlin. This force had to be strong enough to hold out for at least a month, thus winning valuable time in which reinforcements could be sent to Europe and top-level negotiations could be started.

On 25 June 1961, Kennedy made a dramatic TV speech aimed at preparing the American people for the forthcoming international crisis. He said that West Berlin had become the West's touchstone for courage and dedication, reminding the American people of the commitments the US had made to Berlin in 1945 and stressing that these commitments now clashed in principle with the Soviet Union's ambitions. The President explained that he could not let the communists drive the Americans out of Berlin. And summed up by saying that although he was always ready to negotiate, if that would solve the crisis, America must also be ready to defend itself with force if force was used against it.

Kennedy takes measures

On 1 August 1961, exactly one week after the presidential message was televised, the White House's measures were released. So that funds were available to mobilize the US Army, if it became necessary, defense spending in the current fiscal year was increased by more than $3 billion. More than 250,000 US Army reserves were called up, which raised the total strength of America's land forces to over a million men. And, with immediate effect, the US Air Force was to bring 71 squadrons of the ANG and the Air Force Reserve (AFRes) to a state of readiness.

The squadrons affected by the announcement were the 64 ANG squadrons (25,000 men) plus seven squadrons of the AFRes (3,000 men) in a total of 29 States. The Governors of these States were also given the authority to recruit a total of around 5,000 veterans who would be responsible for any training needed to ensure the reservists quickly became proficient — again — with the often complex jet aircraft which had, in the meantime, been put at the disposal of the National and Air Force Reserve. These aircraft were the Republic F-84F Thunderstreak, North American F-86H Sabrejet, North American F-100C Super Sabre and Lockheed F-104A Starfighter and reconnaissance aircraft such as the Republic RF-84F Thunderflash. The transport aircraft mobilized were Boeing C-97A/C Stratofreighters. All in all, the strength of the USAF's Tactical Air Command was to be increased by 650 fighters and 100 transport aircraft.

The East German exodus

In the middle of August the crisis took a dangerous turn. The Soviets began erecting the 'Berlin Wall'.

The Soviets had for years tried to intensify the division between East and West Berlin through psychological and sometimes violent activities. To make movement between the two city sectors more difficult, the Soviets carried out stringent border controls and demanded special travel papers. West Berliners were also prohibited from working in East

Berlin. As more and more measures were implemented and the Soviets, with great regularity, began closing the border crossings, residents of East Germany began to realise that they had gradually become prisoners in their own country. An enormous stream of refugees began to flow towards free West Berlin.

Every week thousands of refugees registered at the receiving centres that had been set up with all speed at the three West Berlin airfields. By the summer of 1961 three and a half million Germans had fled from communism and passed through the Berlin section of the border — the largest gap in the Iron Curtain. In August the threat of war increased the East German population's anxiety about excessive communist oppression and the stream of refugees became a flood: on 9 August the record number of 1,926 refugees arrived in West Berlin. This exodus brought the East German economy to its knees. Not surprising, as thousands of jobs were deserted in the space of just a few months. As a result industrial production stagnated and in several areas threatened to come to a complete halt.

The Kremlin's answer to this flow of refugees was not long coming. During the night of 12/13 August, members of the East German Peoples' Army and Peoples' Police began to close the border crossings with barbed wire and road blocks. Almost simultaneously building began on a meters-high concrete wall that definitively separated the Soviet sector from the other sectors of Berlin. The Berlin Wall became an atrocious barrier of concrete and barbed wire that closed the border between East and West Berlin: the world stood dumbfounded and held its breath.

The highest state of readiness

Kennedy had to accept that building a wall, however inhuman and immoral it was, could not be seen as an act of war on the part of the Soviets. The wall was, moreover, in East German territory which meant the Western Allies could not stop it being built. The wall put an end to West Berlin's role as shop window of the capitalist free West and it shut the escape route to the

West but it did not affect the main goals to which Kennedy held on so tightly; the presence of Western troops in West Berlin, unhindered access to the city and the right of the West Berliners to choose their own political system.

Even so, Kennedy had to react to the new situation, even if it was only a performance that would demonstrate the resolution of the Americans to the people of West Berlin, and he very quickly introduced a number of effective measures. First and foremost he ordered the army command in Europe to send an extra contingent of 1,500 American soldiers to West Berlin. Then he ordered his vice President, Lyndon B. Johnson, to go to West Berlin to show America's continuing support of the people of the city. And finally he ordered that 31 ANG squadrons be designated as Priority Units for possible mobilization. Ten days later ANG headquarters at Andrews AFB near Washington sent the relevant squadrons mobilization notices stating that they would be put on active service as of 1 October 1961 for a period of twelve months. The squadrons were brought to the highest state of readiness and were given exactly thirty days to prepare for what would possibly be a long-term deployment in Europe. The Pentagon issued the 'Move' order on 11 October 1961: eleven ANG Priority Units were sent to Europe to reinforce the USAFE.

USAFE reinforced

The Pentagon sent around 250 fighters to Europe as reinforcements for USAFE: four squadrons of Republic F-84F Thunderstreak fighter-bombers from the Indiana, Missouri, New Jersey and Ohio ANGs, three squadrons of North American F-86H Sabrejet fighter-bombers from the Massachusetts and New York ANGs, three squadrons of Lockheed F-104A Starfighter air defense

A jump into freedom: East German soldier on the run in the Bernauerstrasse just a few days after the borders were closed.
(Landesbildstelle Berlin)

fighters from the Arizona, Tennessee and South Carolina ANGs, and one squadron of Republic RF-84F Thunderflash reconnaissance aircraft from the Alabama ANG. Most squadrons also contained several Lockheed T-33A T-Birds and these aircraft, which were mainly used for communications, were also flown to Europe. For the Pentagon these 'Berlin Deployments' to strengthen the European garrison were an excellent test of the new Rapid Reinforcement tactic.

At the time it was usual for USAF deployments to fly non-stop to European air bases. During the flight the fighters were refuelled several times. The USAF had several squadrons of flying tankers for this purpose. It was a well tested and safe way to fly across the Atlantic Ocean. But the tanker force was too small to handle the large number of aircraft that had to be flown over to Europe within a few days. It was, therefore, decided that the fighters of the Berlin deployments would cross the Atlantic Ocean in the traditional manner. The three F-86H Sabrejet squadrons were the first in line and on 1 and 2 November they departed for their overseas air bases via the Northern 'High Flight' route. Departure point was Goose Bay air base in Canadian Labrador. Stop-overs were made at Sondrastrom (Greenland), Keflavik (Iceland) and Prestwick (Scotland) before a course was set for the European mainland.

Deployment 'Stair Step'

The ANG Squadrons equipped with F-84F Thunderstreak and RF-84F Thunderflash fighters used the southern route via the Lajes air base in the Azores; a route not often used for deployments to Europe. The High Flight route was the safest because there were enough air bases en route that could be used in an emergency. The fighters were also equipped with extra fuel tanks so that during the crossing the pilot almost had sufficient fuel available to be able to turn back or divert to another airport in an emergency.

This was not possible on the Southern route. The distance between the American mainland and the Azores, approximately 2,700 kilometers, was too great. On the way to Lajes the pilots reached a point of no return when the tanks did not contain enough fuel for a successful diversion manoeuvre. In an emergency situation the pilot could only try to fly on. If that was hopeless the only thing he could do was leave his aircraft via the ejection seat.

The five squadrons of F-84Fs assembled at Harmon air base, Newfoundland, Canada, and on 31 October 1961 around a hundred aircraft were on the flight line, ready to take-off for Lajes. To minimize the risk of running out of fuel during the flight (with strong headwind the F-84Fs could not even reach Lajes) the fuel tanks were filled literally to the brim. This was achieved by placing a thirty centimeter wooden block under the aircraft's nosewheel which tilted it slightly backwards enabling several hundred extra litres of fuel to be pumped into the tanks. This simple expedient gave the deployment its name — 'Stair Step'.

At three o'clock in the morning of 1 November the first aircraft received the signal to take-off and begin the crossing. Groups of four aircraft took off at intervals of a few minutes. The entire departure

procedure took a total of over two hours. Flight time to Lajes was over three hours. If fuel consumption was normal the aircraft would arrive with enough fuel for about one hour's flying time still on board. All the aircraft of Deployment Stair Step reached Lajes and a day later most of them took off again for Moron air base, Spain. On 3 November the five squadrons took off one after the other and flew their separate ways to their temporary bases.

Russian jamming stations

The evaluation report on the Stair Step deployment submitted by the Missouri Air National Guard mentions that during their flight to the Canadian Harmon air base the pilots had problems with an annoying high pitched whistling noise on their UHF radios. The phenomenon began during the flight over North Canada and continued for approximately one hour. According to the report the interference technique appeared to be the same as that used by the Germans during World War 2. This incident caused no further problems and was, therefore, not investigated any further. This was not the case with a far more serious incident that occurred during the flight to Lajes. It was caused by misleading radio messages that, suspected the Americans, originated from Russian saboteurs on ship-based radio stations.

For several years the US Navy had had so-called Ocean Station Vessels (OSV) on station in the Atlantic. These floating traffic control centres were equipped with the most up-to-date radio navigation devices and the traffic controllers on board were in continuous contact with American military aircraft above the Atlantic Ocean.

The problems began when OSV *Delta* passed a position report and a faulty course alteration message to Colonel Glennon T. Moran, the leader of the lead flight. Colonel Moran was an experienced pilot and sensible enough to verify the information with OSV *X-Ray* which was stationed further on. It was soon obvious that the position report was wrong. So too was the course alteration which would have taken the entire formation more than one hundred kilometers off its original course.

The other flights also received faulty messages. These resulted in several pilots getting into serious difficulties. One flight of four aircraft followed a faulty course alteration for quite a way, unaware that they were flying in the wrong direction. Their mistake was noticed in the nick of time and was, luckily, corrected. Having used up extra fuel on the diversion the pilots were in severe difficulties on their approach to Lajes which they reached on literally the last drops of kerosene. In fact, later inspection showed that one F-84F had less than a hundred litres of fuel left in its tanks.

Further investigation of these incidents revealed that many Russian trawlers lay along the route. The suspicion was that rather than innocent fishing trawlers these were Soviet Navy 'Okeam' trawlers. These ships were far from innocent; they were equipped with advanced electronic communications equipment and were generally used for monitoring NATO radio traffic at sea and shadowing Western naval vessels. The possibility that American-speaking Russian agents had tried to sabotage the Stair Step deployment by passing false information to the pilots via the OSV radio frequencies could not be ruled out.

The American press carried the story in banner headlines, but the matter was never clarified, nor was the Russians' active involvement ever proven conclusively.

Home Base France

Eight of the eleven deployments were to air bases in France. The Pentagon's choice of French bases was noteworthy to say the least. Just a short while previously French President Charles de Gaulle, not wanting any American nuclear weapons in his country, had expelled all American fighter units. The 180 fighter-bombers of three fighter Wings had to leave. Dismantling the American units took from July 1959 to January 1960. Now, within a few days, de Gaulle would get eight squadrons with a total of nearly two hundred aircraft on his airfields.

These deployments could not have pleased de Gaulle. Within the NATO alliance he had the reputation of being a troublemaker and it was known that he rarely ranged himself behind the American viewpoint. Even in the Berlin conflict his opinions were

Squadrons of the Tactical Air Command were also brought to a state of readiness. From the 479th Tactical Fighter Wing at George Air Force Base, California, a squadron with Lockheed F-104C Starfighters deployed to Moron Air Base in Spain. *(Lockheed)*

directly opposed to the Americans' and, not wanting to co-operate in finding a constructive solution, he torpedoed a NATO resolution for a meeting between the four powers. What de Gaulle wanted, or so it seemed, was to let the Russians do what they wanted in Berlin.

Whether the deployments in France were the Pentagon's way of putting pressure on de Gaulle will never be clear. The French General could not refuse the deployments as this would have meant the irreversible withdrawal of France from NATO. At that moment matters did not go so far.

France was now home base for eight squadrons of fighters. Several weeks before their own arrival supplies and equipment began arriving. American cargo ships sailed into the harbours of St Nazaire, La Rochelle and La Pallice. In addition, a large number of Military Air Transport Service (MATS) transports landed at the American air base at Chateauroux in central France. The material and equipment was destined for six airfields, most of which were in eastern France. The four F-84F Thunderstreak squadrons (166th TFS Ohio ANG, 163rd TFS Indiana ANG, 110th TFS Missouri ANG and 141st TFS New Jersey ANG) went respectively to the air bases Etain-Rouvres, Chambley, Toul-Rosières and Chaumont-Semoutiers. The three F-86F Sabrejet squadrons (101st TFS and 131st TFS Massachusetts ANG and 138th TFS New York ANG) were stationed at Phalsbourg-Bourscheid air base, while the RF-84F Thunderflash reconnaissance aircraft of the 106th TRS Alabama ANG went to Dreux-Semonches near Paris.

★　★　★

Starfighters by air freight

The Berlin Deployment also gave the USAF an opportunity to test a new method of flying combat aircraft to Europe. This time the aircraft did not fly to their European air bases under their own power but were airlifted in Douglas C-124 Globemaster IIs.

The MATS' colossal C-124 transports had already been used to airlift jet fighters and their support equipment in August 1958 during the Formosa (now Taiwan) crisis. After Chinese communists, supported by Russia, had partitioned the islands of Quemoy and Matsu and threatened to occupy them, the Pentagon decided to send a squadron of Lockheed F-104A Starfighters to Formosa to support the US Pacific Air Force.

At the time it was usual to ship combat aircraft over such distances on aircraft carriers which took at least several weeks, time that was not available in the Formosa crisis. For this reason C-124s were brought in to fly the F-104s over to the Ching Chuan Kang air base on Formosa. This method was to be used again during the Berlin crisis.

Once again it was F-104 Starfighters that had to be airlifted. The first aircraft sent to Europe by this method came from the 157th FIS of the South Carolina ANG. On Friday, 10 November 1961, the first F-104s were loaded into the MATS' C-124s at McEntire AFB. To make loading easier the aircraft were partly dismantled; wings, tail and nose sections were removed.

A 'Greek Party' Boeing KC-97L during air refuelling of an 81st TFW F-4C Phantom over Southern Germany. *(Collection Cees Steijger)*

transferred from SAC to the USAFE. From April 1966 the USAFE had control of the Spanish air bases of Zaragoza and Moron as well as Torrejon, near Madrid, where the 16th Air Force was headquartered. It was to these airfields that the 401st TFW with its three squadrons of F-100 Super Sabres was posted in the spring of 1966. The 16th Air Force also gradually took over responsibility for all USAFE operations around the Mediterranean.

In addition there was the so-called TUSLOG organization. TUSLOG (Turkish US Logistics Group) was established in 1955 to support the Turkish armed forces and the USAFE's activities in Turkey and was headquartered in Ankara, TUSLOG's Detachment 10

The Boeing KB-50 was too slow. *(MAP)*

at Incirlik Air Base near Adana supported the USAFE's training activities and lent a hand to the SAC, which in the 1960s used Incirlik intensively as a base for U-2 reconnaissance flights along the Soviet border and in the Middle East. (Incirlik was also a former Forward Operational Location of the CIA.)

Crested Cap

On 2 May 1967 the US Department of Defense announced that due to the loss of the French bases, the 49th TFW's three squadrons at Spangdahlem and the 417th TFS of the 50th TFW at Hahn plus several thousands of the troops stationed in West Germany would be recalled to the US. Although the squadrons were relocated to the US, they were still part of the USAFE's permanent force. According to the Pentagon this new strategy followed the so-called dual–basing principle which meant that the squadrons in the US were held in such a state of readiness that they could return to their European bases at any given moment without lengthy preparations being necessary.

During 1967 the 49th TFW's three squadrons flew back to the US where they were stationed at Holloman AFB in New Mexico. According to Beatrice la Liu, the 50th TFW's Wing Historian, the 417th TFS did not return to the US until 1968. The squadron was stationed at Mountain Home AFB in Idaho. In 1968 the four squadrons switched over completely to McDonnell Douglas F-4D fighter-bombers and then undertook intensive preparations for their new role within the USAFE. The primary task of the four dual-based squadrons was to carry out Project 'Crested

The introduction of the McDonnell Douglas F-4 Phantom was accelerated in 1969. *(Ton van Schaik)*

Cap', an annual exercise in which they returned to their European bases for several weeks of intensive exercises.

The first Crested Cap deployment was held in January 1969. At the beginning of the month the 49th TFW's three squadrons were flown from Holloman AFB to Spangdahlem air base while the 417th TFS went to Hahn. At the same time as the first 'Crested Cap' exercise was taking place, the USAREUR (US Army in Europe) was holding its large-scale 'Reforger' exercise, for the first time, in West Germany.

Reforger, an acronym of REturn FORces to GERmany, is an exercise in which a large number of troops is moved from the US to Europe in a very short period of time. It is an annual test of the rapid reinforcement of American ground forces in Europe and also acts as a Flexible Response demonstration. Reforger is a typical army exercise in which the sea

Soviet tanks in Czechoslovakia: the Prague Spring was rudely disturbed. *(ANP)*

and air supply lines are tested. Most of the heavy equipment such as armoured vehicles, artillery, etc, is shipped; the troops are flown to Europe. Crested Cap, by contrast, is a purely air force affair and must be seen as the USAFE's equivalent of Reforger.

★ ★ ★

'Greek Party': refuelling in the air

As the USAFE acquired more up-to-date jet fighters like the F-100 Super Sabres and the F-101 Voodoos, etc, all of which had air refuelling capabilities, 'filling up', in the air became part of the daily routine. Since the middle of the 1950s the USAFE had its own Air Refuelling Squadron (ARS) to do the job. This squadron, the 420th ARS, was stationed at Sculthorpe air base in Norfolk, England, and was equipped with Boeing KB-50 Superfortress tankers. As well as four powerful piston engines these converted bombers had two extra J-47 jet engines that enabled the tanker to match the speed with the faster jet fighters during refuelling. But most of the KB-50s were more than fifteen years old and too slow to refuel the faster jet fighters such as the F-4 Phantom. For this reason the squadron was disbanded on 25 May 1964 and from then on the USAFE's refuelling function was taken over by SAC's much faster jet-engined KC-135 Stratotankers.

At that time, developments in the Vietnam War had led to a large number of SAC's KC-135s being stationed at bases in Thailand, Guam and Okinawa. The USAFE's refuelling operations suffered as a consequence and reached an absolute low when, at the beginning of 1965, the US Defense Secetary, Robert McNamara, gave the go-ahead for operation 'Arc Light', the collective name for the B-52 bombardment of North Vietnam.. It did not appear as if the situation would improve for some time.

General Maurice A. Preston, Commander of USAFE, saw that he would have to call on the air refuelling squadrons of the Air National Guard. At that time the ANG had five squadrons equipped with Boeing KC-97L Stratofreighter tankers. Like the KB-50J these aircraft were fitted with two extra J-47 jet engines. On 1 May 1967, after a short and successful evaluation period during which the KC-97's capabilities of refuelling F-4 Phantoms was tested, ANG headquarters at Andrews AFB near Washington sent four KC-97s from the 181st ARS (Texas ANG) to Rhein Main. This operation was code-named 'Greek Party' and entailed the rotational temporary detachment of four ANG KC-97s at a time. During their rotational deployment, which lasted several weeks, the KC-97s flew an average of two missions a day (during the period 1970-1973 this frequency increased to six missions a day).

The USAFE used two tanking methods, the probe and drogue method and the now much used flying boom method. The difference between the methods is that with the probe and drogue method the pilot of the tanking aircraft must make contact with the funnel the tanker deploys on the end of a flexible hose, while the flying boom method uses filler tube that is manoeuvred from the tanker. The probe and drogue method is now used mainly by the US Navy and the US Marine Corps. The USAFE's modern fighters (F-16, F-15 and F-111) can only be refuelled via a flying boom.

In the first two years of Greek Party, the ANG's KC-97s crossed the Atlantic a total of more than 500 times. Although Greek Party was set up as an interim solution it continued until 1977. Over the ten years the KC-97s flew 7,000 missions and made 47,000 hook-ups during which a total of 100 million litres of kerosene was transferred. In 1977 the KC-97s' job was taken over by KC-135s of the European Tanker Task Force which was stationed at Mildenhall and Fairford.

★   ★   ★

The invasion of Czechoslovakia

1968 brought great changes for the Czechoslovakian people. Prominent reformist communists, led by Alexander Dubcek, wanted to replace Soviet socialism with a more humane socialism. They were, however, stopped.

On 21 August 1968 the Russian press bureau TASS announced that Soviet Army units, together with units from the GDR, Bulgaria, Hungary and Poland, had crossed into Czechoslovakian territory. TASS reported that this military intervention must put a stop to a situation that threatened the existing socialist regime in Czechoslovakia. The further worsening of conditions in Czechoslovakia would, according to the Kremlin's mouthpiece, affect the interests of the Soviet Union and the other Eastern Bloc countries and threaten the security of the Socialist Bloc.

And that was, at the same time, a threat to the foundations of European peace.

In the early morning of Wednesday, 21 August 1968,

the armored cars and tanks of the five Warsaw Pact countries rumbled into Prague. Shortly after, First Secretary of the Czechoslovakian Communist Party, Dubcek, and several of his political advisors were taken away to prison in Moscow. The Prague Spring of far-reaching reforms which had begun eight months before and which was to herald a new era of Czechoslovakian communism was over. The Prague variation was to have been a remodelled socialism that put an end to the communist dictatorship. In the eyes of the communist leaders of neighbouring states this could not be allowed. In particular, the Russian leader Leonid Brezhnev, the Polish Party Chairman Wladyslaw Gomulka and the Chairman of the East German Communist Party Walter Ulbricht, feared that the introduction of the Prague variation of socialism in the other Eastern Bloc countries would eventually lead to their own deposition.

Under heavy pressure Dubcek and his progressive colleagues signed a protocol that blocked the route to liberalization and that irrevocably reversed all reforms (such as the restoration of the communist censure).

Reticent reactions

The sharpest condemnation of the military invasion of Czechoslovakia came from the communist countries of China, Rumania and Albania, which even went so far as to secede from the Warsaw Pact a few months later. The West, in contrast, was indignant but extremely reticent. As fierce as the US's reaction had been before and during the Berlin crisis in 1961 and as hard as the US's response had been to Russia's attempted siting of nuclear missiles on Cuba in 1962, the US's reaction to events in Czechoslovakia was now very reserved.

Possibly President Johnson valued the good relationship with Russia and did not want a serious political confrontation between East and West. Perhaps he was looking ahead to the US-Russia SALT (Strategic Arms Limitation) talks due to be held in Helsinki at the end of 1969 and for which preparations were already in full swing. In any case, what was the alternative?

The West had to remain passive. The Kremlin would have considered anything else an interference with the internal affairs of a Warsaw Pact country. Direct intervention from the West in a situation that affected communism so deeply would in all probability soon have led to another world war.

According to Dr Charles Hildreth, former USAFE historian, however, there was, in fact, a far-reaching reaction in the sense that the Pentagon wanted to push ahead with the modernization of the USAFE and gave orders for accelerated introduction of the McDonnell F-4 Phantom. In addition, a second Tactical Airlift Wing was formed (the former 322nd AD was renamed the 322nd TAW and stationed at Rhein Main) which provided additional capability for fast reinforcement of the USAFE and US Army troops in West Germany. The Pentagon also decided to supply the 20th TFW at Upper Heyford air base in England with 82 advanced General Dynamics F-111 fighters. A decision which, it is true, came more than a year after the Prague Spring, but a decision which must be seen in the light of the turbulent political developments that took place at the end of the 1960s.

Chapter 7
The USAFE's style of the seventies

At the start of the 1970s there was certainly no shortage of self confidence in America. The boost to national morale of twice landing on the moon during the second half of 1969 was generally considered a fair return for the billions spent on the Apollo project.

It was a different story in Vietnam where all America had to show for an annual investment of tens of billions of dollars was an enormous loss: of materials — helicopters, vehicles, tanks — and, far more painful, of thousands of American lives.

Continuing the fight in Vietnam cost the Americans dear. In 1970 the US Army had around half a million troops in South-East Asia while the USAF had hundreds of combat aircraft, bombers and transporters dispersed across its many bases in South Vietnam, Thailand and the Philippines. Add to this the many US Navy and US Marine Corps units that were involved and it becomes clear just how heavy a burden America's involvement was for the national budget. Reason enough for Congress to begin taking a critical look at the US's world-wide military obligations late in the 1960s.

As far as the USAFE was concerned this added up to a steady decrease in personnel strength and number of aircraft. In 1961 the USAFE had nearly 100,000 personnel and around 1,600 aircraft. Since that time America's escalating involvement in the Vietnam War had resulted in a steady decrease in the size of the USAFE's organization. In 1970 — the year the organization celebrated its silver jubilee — the figures were just 57,000 personnel and 770 aircraft. Despite this considerable reduction, the USAFE's qualitative strength remained high. An extensive modernization programme had begun in the 1960s with the introduction of the McDonnell Douglas F-4 Phantom. The new decade, born under this star of modernization, would see the introduction of the new General Dynamics F-111 combat aircraft, McDonnell Douglas F-15 air superiority fighter and Fairchild A-10 ground attack

fighter, all aircraft that heralded a new style — the style of the 1970s.

Swingwings to England

Seldom has an aircraft design so preoccupied the minds of the US military as the General Dynamics F-111. The F-111, like the expensive North American XB-70 Valkyrie, began as a highly controversial and money-hungry project. While XB-70 was cancelled development of the F-111 continued.

The F-111 was General Dynamics' winning entry in the 1962 TFX (Tactical Fighter Experimental) competition held by the American Department of Defense with the aim of producing a new tactical fighter for both the USAF and the US Navy. General Dynamics was to build the F-111A for the US Air Force while Grumman was sub-contracted to build the F-111B for the US Navy.

A unique feature of the F-111 is its variable sweep wing, or swingwing as it was popularly called, which is still acknowledged as a technical *tour de force*. In spread position the wing provides maximum lift at minimum speed — an advantage during take-off and while flying at low altitude. In swept-back position the wing offers only minimum resistance and that is ideal for supersonic flight.

The F-111 was awaited with bated breath, because the F-111A was to replace the F-4s and F-105 (development began in 1960 to replace the F-105!) and the F-111B, the Navy's Vought F-8 Crusaders and Douglas F-6 Skyrays. On 15 October 1964, during the roll-out ceremony at Fort Worth, Texas, Defense Secretary Robert McNamara remarked enthusiastically that the F-111 was faster than the best fighters at the time and had a firepower equal to five World War 2 Boeing B-17s. 'For the first time in the history of the air force we have an aircraft with the range of a transport aircraft, the weapons capacity of a bomber and the manoeuvrability of a fighter,' said McNamara to the assembled press.

Above: A Douglas EB-66E of the 39th TEWS photographed at Spangdahlem Air Base, Germany. A great many antennas can be clearly seen under the fuselage. *(Ton van Schaik)*

Opposite: After a difficult start, the General Dynamics F-111 became the best penetration fighter of the US Air Force. *(General Dynamics)*

Unfortunately, technical problems arose during the ensuing test programme. The F-111B suffered because of an increase in all-up weight of the aircraft. In April 1965 the DoD placed an order for 431 F-111As and 24 F-111Bs. In 1964 an order for 24 F-111Cs was placed by the Australian Air Force and the Royal Air Force ordered 50 F-111K versions. A further 76 FB-111As went to SAC.

The F-111 project continued to be dogged by setbacks. The aircraft had a weight problem, for example — the prototype weighed 40,000 kilos; eight tons heavier than originally intended. Which was one of the reasons why the F-111, instead of being the fast and manoeuvrable multi-role fighter it was supposed to be was, in fact, useless as an air defense fighter — its most vital task — and only suitable as a bomber.

The US Navy dropped the F-111B project in July 1968. opting instead for the very promising Grumman F-14 Tomcat which also had a variable wing. The Royal Air Force cancelled its order in January 1968. The USAF went ahead as planned and in 1967 accepted the first production versions into service. These first F-111A's went to the 474th TFW at Cannon AFB, New Mexico in October 1967.

Gradually the shortcomings were rectified and improvements were incorporated into later versions such as the F-111E and the F-111F. In 1969, the Pentagon decided to send F-111s to England.

The 20th TFW at RAF Upper Heyford took 79 F-111Fs into service. When the first aircraft arrived in September 1970, an intensive familiarization programme for both pilots and ground crew was set into motion. During that winter most of the 20th TFW's pilots were trained on the F-111. In November 1971, General David C Jones, Commander, USAFE, declared the 20th operational.

★   ★   ★

Flying jamming stations

The USAF has always had several squadrons of special aircraft at its disposal for electronic warfare. These aircraft, brimming with advanced electronic systems, serve primarily as flying jamming stations. At the end of the 1960s the USAFE also acquired such flying jamming stations, in this case Douglas EB-66E Destroyers. The EB-66Es were flown by the 39th Tactical Early Warning Squadron (TEWS) which was stationed at Spangdahlem and Bitburg air bases.

To enable them to perform in various capacities rather than just as jamming stations, the aircraft carried a comprehensive (for the time) arsenal of electronics including UHF/VHF radio receivers and transmitters and were recognisable by the large array of antennas under the fuselage. This electronic equipment was used on ELINT missions along the Eastern Bloc borders. In addition, the EB-66s frequently carried out Electronic Counter-Measures (ECM) missions during which active radar jammers were used to transmit disruptive signals in the hostile radar systems' GHz band. In effect, it was rather like throwing an electronic spanner in the works.

Around 1970, Martin EB-57Es were also seen in Europe. These aircraft belonged to several Defense Systems Evaluation Squadrons (DSES) which formed part of the then Air Defense Command. Official USAFE History Office documents reveal that one EB-57E squadron came functionally under the USAFE. This was certainly the 17th DSES from Malmstrom AFB, Montana. The squadron's EB-57Es generally visited Europe several times a year to participate in NATO exercises.

the bank of the River Jordan. Israel, squeezed on both sides, almost succumbed to the Arab superiority. On 8 October a desperate Moshe Dayan, Israel's Minister of Defense, said that the way and the Jewish state could both be lost. He had solid grounds for his fears. On the Sinai front Egyptian forces had grown to around 100,000 personnel with roughly 1,100 tanks while in the north Syria had 75,000 troops and 140 tanks. The Israeli army was up against vastly superior forces on two fronts and, this time, could not depend on the Heyl Ha'Avir, the Israeli air force, that had ensured success during the Six-Day War by totally destroying the Egyptian air force before it entered the fray. Now the Arab air defense included modern Russian mobile SA-6 Gainful and SA-7 Grail surface-to-air missiles. The Israeli air force was no longer master in the air and even lost a large number of aircraft in the first days of the war.

More aircraft for Israel

Almost immediately it became aware of how dire the situation was for the Israelis, the American Congress decided to supply military aid to Israel. According to an article published in the American journal *Wings of Gold* in 1979, initial US support included Lockheed C-130 Hercules transporters, McDonnell Douglas F-4E Phantoms (some from the 4th TFW at Seymour Johnson AFB, North Carolina) and Douglas A-4 Skyhawks. All told, twelve Hercules and around 150 fighters were supplied to Israel in a very short space of time. Delivery began in the middle of October and continued for some time.

During their ferry flight to Israel the fighters were

Each year the 17th Defense Systems Evaluation Squadron deployed its Martin EB-57Es to Europe. *(Collection Cees Steijger)*

refuelled over the Atlantic and the Mediterranean by KC-135s. On arrival at their Israeli base they were quickly prepared for action. Observers on the scene reported that some of the F-4Es went into action within hours of arriving from the US.

Some of the A-4 Skyhawks were ferried to Israel in a totally different way; their refuelling stops were on American 6th Fleet aircraft carriers sailing around the Azores (USS *Kennedy*), south of Spain (USS *Roosevelt*) and around Crete (USS *Independence*). The Military Airlift Command also used Lockheed C-141 Starlifter and C-5 Galaxy heavy transport aircraft for an extensive airlift set up to keep the Israeli forces supplied with tanks, ammunition, anti-tank weapons, helicopters, etc. Due partly to this reinforcement and partly to the fact that the Arab armies ran out of supplies, the tide soon turned. The Israelis retook the Golan Heights and then turned their attention to the Sinai.

Sensational news

In the west Israel was under heavy pressure from a strong Egyptian army that had consolidated its positions in the Sinai and feared an Egyptian invasion. The fourth Arab-Israeli war threatened to get completely out of hand. According to the CIA, Israel was covertly fitting nuclear warheads to its Jericho ground-target rockets at a secret location somewhere around Dimona in the Negev desert. As a last resort, Israel would use these nuclear weapons for strikes on Cairo and Damascus.

William Kennedy's book *The Intelligence War* published in England in 1983 contains remarkable details

A F-4E Phantom of the 4th TFW during a Crested Cap deployment to Ramstein in the seventies. Several F-4Es that the Pentagon supplied to Israel came directly from the 4th TFW. *(Collection Cees Steijger)*

about this situation. In the chapter 'Intelligence and the war in the air', it states that around 13 October 1973 a Lockheed SR-71 Blackbird spyplane from the USAF's 9th Strategic Reconnaissance Wing was used to obtain irrefutable proof of the CIA's claim. The SR-71 took-off from a base in Florida (Homestead AFB?) for a non-stop flight to the Middle East. The aircraft was refuelled en route by KC-135s probably originating from Torrejon air base in Spain. It entered Israeli airspace at high altitude, thus remaining beyond the reach of Israeli air defense (the Israeli air force, according to reports, tried in vain to intercept it with two F-4Es). Over the Negev Desert the SR-71 managed to take razor-sharp photographs of the activity around Dimona.

Nixon telephones Brezhnev

The spy flight was a success; the photographs proved conclusively that the Israeli army was siting nuclear Jericho rockets. This news dropped like a bombshell on the White House. President Nixon, on the advice of the National Security Council, contacted the Russian Party Leader Leonid Brezhnev on the hot-line in an attempt to prevent the affair escalating into a world conflict. He succeeded. The world leaders agreed to bring the situation in the Middle East back into balance. At least, according to *The Intelligence War* that can be assumed from the fact that during the evening of 13 October 1973 a Russian cargo ship left the Nicolaev Marine Base at Odessa with an unknown number of nuclear warheads on board.

If, as is likely, these warheads were for converting the Russian SS-1 Scud conventional surface-to-surface missiles deployed around Cairo and the Aswan Dam, it would have resulted in the conflicting parties having around twenty nuclear missiles each. This would have restored the military balance and, however paradoxical it may sound, reduced the risk of a nuclear conflict. At the same time, the Israeli army began to prevail so there was no longer a danger of an Egyptian invasion and with it a nuclear strike.

An alarming crisis

At the end of the Arab-Israeli war another alarming crisis arose unexpectedly. After the UN Security Council called for a ceasefire on 22 October 1973, it seemed that peace would soon be restored. There were minor truce infringements by both sides but then, suddenly, Israeli troops advanced. Sadat, the Egyptian President, called on both the US and the Soviet Union to send a combined force to enforce compliance with the UN ceasefire.

The Kremlin announced that if the US did not wish to join in a combined expedition the Soviet army was ready to go in on its own and, according to CIA reports, the Soviet Union was indeed preparing to send several army battalions to Egypt. In addition, the Russian fleet in the Mediterranean was reinforced. On receiving this information the White House put US forces throughout the world on military alert. This 'defense condition three' was a drastic measure intended to make clear to the Soviet leaders in Moscow that the US was now in earnest and that the Red Army's intervention in the Middle East would not be tolerated.

Above: Boeing EC-135H Looking Glass of the 10th ACCS on approach to Mildenhall Air Base. *(Cees Steijger)*

Top: Boeing EC-135H Looking Glass of the 10th ACCS departing from Mildenhall Air Base. *(Collection Dick van der Aart)*

The system works as follows. The downed pilot has a 130 meter-long nylon cable with a deflated helium balloon attached to one end. He fastens the other end of the cable to his special safety suit, inflates the helium balloon and releases it. The C-130 flies in at around 150 km/h and positions the hooks, which look rather like scissors being opened. The balloon is caught between the hooks and the pilot is hoisted into the air and then winched on board. The recovery system was not generally known about until around 1965 when several C-130s went into action in the Vietnam War. Being also equipped with terrain following radar and a vast amount of ECM equipment, these special EC-130E-1 Skyhooks were ideally suited for dropping infiltrators and agents behind enemy lines and picking them up again.

This, then, was the type of aircraft used in Europe by the 7th SOS as MC-130E Combat Talons. Although even today very little is known about this special unit, the mere fact that the USAF information service always answers 'no comment' to any questions about its role is sufficient to allow the tentative conclusion that clandestine operations are involved.

One corner of the shroud of mystery was lifted by the Information Department of the 1st Special Operations Wing stationed at Hurlburt Field in Florida. This Wing includes the 8th SOS which has a similar role to the 7th SOS at Rhein Main and, in addition, is responsible for the training of all USAF Special Operations pilots. According to a Fact Sheet issued by the 1st SOW, the MC-130Es can now be used for infiltration operations in which commando and sabotage units are dropped in enemy territory and for difficult air drops. These drops are often from an extremely low altitude; during the past few years drops from below fifteen meters have not been exceptional.

The 7th SOS's MC-130Es have been spotted in every corner of Europe. These sightings have perhaps been connected with NATO marine unit exercises with which the 7th SOS is also involved. One of the most bizarre sightings dates from January 1976 when a traveller from West Berlin saw a low-flying C-130 over the Transitstrasse, the transit route, near Magdeburg in the DDR. Flying at an estimated fifty meters over the motorway, the Hercules disappeared northwards at great speed. It was certainly an MC-130E from the 7th SOS but what it was doing in the DDR is not so certain. Granted it was flying perfectly legally in the air corridor at the time of the sighting, the fact that it was a black MC-130E from the mysterious 7th SOS does make one a trifle suspicious.

A sinister reputation

The US Air Force's Lockheed U-2 spy planes' European operations were also shrouded in the necessary mystery. For many years the USAF managed to keep its use of the U-2s in Europe secret. But when a U-2C crashed on the German ski resort of Winterberg on 29 May 1975, the silence surrounding the U-2 operations was broken in one loud bang. The unhappy U-2C, serial number *56-6700*, was one of two U-2s stationed at Wetherfield air base, England, where the almost unknown 66th Combat Support Squadron was housed. The two aircraft belonged to the 100th Strategic Reconnaissance Wing at Davis-Monthan in Arizona and, while it was common knowledge that the 100th SRW usually had U-2 detachments stationed at Osan air base in Korea and U-Tapao in Thailand, practically nothing was known about its European operations.

In his book *Aerial Espionage*, the Dutch aviation writer Dick van der Aart writes that during the first half of the 1970s U-2s from the U-Tapao were used for communications intelligence missions (COMINT) along the Chinese border. According to official communiqués, the same U-2 spy planes came to Europe in 1975 to test a new system to localize Soviet radars. This was the new Airborne Locator Strike System with which the RF-4C reconnaissance aircraft were equipped several years later. What was remarkable was that rather than their normal matt black paint these aircraft sported a friendly blue/grey camouflage scheme. This colour scheme later became known as Broken-Sky.

According to several sources, this change was made at the special request of the British government which wanted to do something about the black U-2's sinister reputation. England was always a desirable departure point for American espionage missions. The first U-2s were observed in 1956 at Lakenheath air base, not by the 'experts' but by young aircraft spotters.

Strike Force, British aviation writer Robert Jackson's book about the USAFE in England since 1948, contains some interesting facts about U-2 operations in England. During 1957 the U-2s stationed at Lakenheath were used for spy flights over the Soviet Union. One of them was the U-2, serial number *56-6689*, in which CIA agent Francis Gary Powers was shot down over the Russian armaments centre at Sverdlovsk in May 1960.

Reconnaissance centre Mildenhall

For quite some years now most SAC air traffic has gone to Mildenhall air base, England — headquarters of the 3rd Air Force. In the 1970s SAC traffic (EC-135s, RC-135s and later also U-2s and SR-71s) increased so much that Mildenhall's importance grew until it became known as SAC's European Reconnaissance centre.

The 513th Tactical Airlift Wing has been housed at this former RAF Bomber Command base since 1966. Until 1976 it was responsible for operations of the approximately twenty Military Airlift Command C-130s that at any time were stationed at Mildenhall on a temporary 65-day posting. Nowadays, the MAC is directly responsible for these temporary duty deployments. The 513th TAW is still responsible for operations of four Boeing EC-135H 'Looking Glass' Flying Command Posts of the 10th Airborne Command and Control Squadron (ACCS).

Mildenhall became even more important when it became the base for the SAC KC-135 Stratotankers that were used for the growing number of TAC deployments to USAFE European bases. At first these KC-135s still belonged to Detachment One of the SAC's 98th Strategic Wing at Torrejon air base, Spain. Later all SAC operations, including Detachment One, came under the SAC 7th Air Division which was headquartered at Ramstein. The 7th Air Division also became responsible for the KC-135s of the Strategic Squadron at Zaragoza, Spain, and the 11th Strategic Group of the European Tanker Task Force (ETTF) at Fairford, England. In addition, the 7th Air Division co-ordinated the RC-135 ELINT/Comint operations of both the 922nd Support Squadron at Hellenikon air base, Athens and the 306th Strategic Wing at Mildenhall.

For many years strange and bizarre types of Boeing RC-135 reconnaissance aircraft have been observed

The Lockheed U-2C looked harmless in the blue/grey 'Broken Sky' camouflage colours. *(Lockheed)*

regularly at Mildenhall. Most of these aircraft come from the 55th Strategic Reconnaissance Wing at Offutt AFB, Nebraska. Among the most striking, and easily recognizable, are the Boeing RC-135U/V/W aircraft with their numerous blade antennas under the fuselage and their large cheeks on either side of the forward fuselage section. Behind these cheeks the RC-135 carries an advanced Side Looking Airborne Radar (SLAR) with which it can receive radar and radio signals from far behind the borders of, for example, the Eastern Bloc. And that is also the primary function of these four-engined reconnaissance aircraft. From Mildenhall the RC-135s fly ELINT and COMINT missions along the borders of Poland, the Soviet Union and Czechoslovakia. The twenty or so specialists on board the RC-135s during such missions listen to and tape military radio frequencies and communications.

Strategic reconnaissance

For strategic reconnaissance the 9th Strategic Reconnaissance Wing at Beale AFB, California, had two squadrons; one of Lockheed SR-71A 'Blackbirds' (11th SRS) and one of Lockheed U-2/TR-1s (99th SRS). These sky-spies were by no means strangers to Europe. U-2s have been in Europe since the 1950s. The majority have operated from support posts in England (Brize Norton, Upper Heyford and Mildenhall) or from bases in Germany (Wiesbaden and Ramstein) although U-2s have also usually been stationed at Bodo in northern Norway. For reconnaissance along the Eastern Bloc borders in southern Europe, U-2 missions have flown from remote fields in Turkey (Incirlik, for example) while the British Akrotiri airfield on Cyprus was often the departure point for missions over the Middle East.

Above: Boeing RC-135V of the 55th Strategic Reconnaissance Wing photographed at Mildenhall in 1976. *(Cees Steijger)*

Top: F-15 Eagle of the 22nd TFS uses its large airbrake while on finals to Bitburg Air Base, Germany. *(Henk Koerts)*

'The Range' — at Groom Dry Lake in the Nevada desert, but no hard evidence.

Without a doubt the SR-71 was among America's most advanced military aircraft. According to official SAC figures it could reach a cruising speed of more than Mach 3 and a height of 80,000 feet (24 km). According to the trade press the aircraft could do far more with the almost 30,000 kg of thrust provided by its two Pratt & Whitney J-58 turbo-ramjets. To achieve the SR-71's phenomenal performance a number of special features were necessary. The aircraft was made almost entirely of Beta B-120 titanium, which can resist the high temperatures that result from friction at high speeds (at 3,300 km/h the fuselage temperature is more than 650°C).

As is usual with the USAF's reconnaissance aircraft, precise details of the SR-71's equipment and operation have never been officially released. There is not a shadow of doubt that the SR-71 was used for a wide range of electronic reconnaissance purposes such as ELINT and COMINT missions. In the trade press the SR-71 is often mentioned in conjunction with LOROP cameras (Long Range Oblique Photograph) which can register an object the size of a football at a distance of 100 kilometers. Fitted with this type of camera and flying at a height of 24 kilometers, the SR-71 could photograph an area of 259,000 square kilometers in just one hour. SR-71s remained in service until the end of 1989, when

the US Department of Defense, for budgetary reasons, decided to cease operations with the SR-71.

Eagle ideal for air superiority

In 1976 the modernization of the USAF went a stage further with the introduction of the advanced McDonnell Douglas F-15A Eagle air superiority fighter.

The F-15A design stemmed from the mid-1960s when far-sighted military planners in the Pentagon came to the conclusion that a new air defense fighter was needed, and quickly, as an answer to new Soviet air defense fighters.

Although the McDonnell Douglas F-4 Phantom was equipped with modern infra red-guided Sidewinder and radar-controlled Sparrow air-to-air missiles, it often proved no match for the manoeuvrable MiG-19 Farmer and MiG-21 Fishbed fighters in Vietnam. One reason was the young American pilots' lack of air combat experience. Another was that while the F-4 was an ideal platform for a great variety of weapons and suitable for an equal number of different tasks, it had not been developed as a dedicated air superiority fighter.

The USAF's last real air superiority fighter was the North American F-86 Sabre that had been lord and master of the air during the Korean War. The American F-86 pilots were nicknamed 'MiG-killers' and in the period 1950-1953 shot down at least 792 MiGs, most of which were MiG-15 Fagot fighters — the Russian showpiece of the communist North Korean Air Force. America's own losses were only 78 Sabres. At the heart of this success lay the F-86's remarkable flight characteristics. The F-86 was not only fast, it had exceptional acceleration and it was extremely manoeuvrable even under difficult conditions. The F-86 was built for air combat and all its best features were echoed in the McDonnell Douglas F-15A Eagle.

The Soviet Union's new MiG and Sukhoi fighters made the American military anxious. The MiG-25 Foxbat made them pull out all the stops to get the F-15A.

Phenomenal performer

American intelligence reports about the MiG-25 left little room for comfort; the performance of this latest Russian combat aircraft was far superior to any American aircraft. The twin-engined MiG-25 reached speeds of over 3,000 km/h even at high altitude (over 70,000 feet) and it could be armed with radar-guided AA-6 Acrid air-to-air missiles. When the Soviets stationed large numbers in the Soviet Union and later in the GDR, the American Department of Defense had a problem. The solution had to be provided by the McDonnell Douglas F-15A. Just like the MiG-25 it has two powerful engines and a double tail fin. But that was where the similarity ends.

The Foxbat is a formidable performer, but the F-15A is phenomenal. Its two powerful Pratt & Whitney F-100 turbofans each provide a thrust of around 12,500 kg. And with full tanks and armed with four AIM-7F Sparrow air-to-air missiles the F-15A's take-off weight of around 20,000 kg gives a thrust/weight ratio better than 1:1. This is the basis of the Eagle's phenomenal performance; performance that still keeps the aviation world standing open-mouthed in amazement. At the

The SR-71 was one of the most advanced aircraft of the USAF.
(Lockheed)

beginning of February 1975, as part of project 'Streak Eagle', the F-15A broke no less than eight world climbing records. During one record attempt the Eagle broke the sound barrier nineteen seconds after the start then, climbing vertically, broke through the magical Mach 2 threshold in just two minutes. After a climb of just three and a half minutes, the F-15A was thirty kilometers up. The eagle had truly soared and demonstrated it was a fully fledged air superiority fighter — just too late, it is true, to be able to play any significant role in Vietnam, but ready to considerably strengthen Europe's air defense.

'Ready Eagle'

The F-15A was deployed to Germany in April 1972 with the 36th TFW.

From April 1972 to 1983 all F-4 wings were replaced by F-15 and F-16 fighters. 36th TFW's existing F-4E Phantoms were incorporated into three new USAFE squadrons which were established at Hahn (313th TFS), Spangdahlem (480th TFS) and Ramstein (512th TFS). Preparations for the switch to the F-15 went ahead at full speed. Its introduction to the USAFE was given the project name 'Ready Eagle' and, naturally, included transition training for the USAFE pilots.

This retraining was the joint responsibility of the USAFE and TAC and first began in January 1976 at Langley AFB, Virginia, where the 1st TFW, was stationed.

At Langley the USAFE's future F-15 pilots were given a crash course that familiarized them with the new aircraft in a relatively short time. The first F-15A's arrived at Bitburg on 7 January 1977. These were two TF-15A trainers (serial numbers *75-049* and *75-050*), that had flown non-stop from Langley in seven and a half hours. These Eagles were to be used primarily for ground crew familiarization in anticipation of the arrival of the 525th TFS's first F-15As. The 23 aircraft for this first operational squadron left Langley on 27 April 1977 for a mass Atlantic crossing. Over the Atlantic, the Eagles were refuelled by eight KC-135s and one KC-135 from the New Hampshire ANG; the tankers of the mass deployment all landed successfully at Mildenhall. Over the following months the aircraft for two other squadrons (22nd TFS and 53rd TFS) arrived. The 36th TFW's full strength of 79 fully-operational F-15As was reached in December 1977. Project Ready Eagle was completed in precisely one year.

Above: Lockheed U-2R spy planes often operated from Akrotiri Air Base, Cyprus, for reconnaissance missions over the Middle East. *(Collection Cees Steijger)*

Top: With its characteristic double fin tails and its two powerful engines, the F-15 is a real master of the sky. *(US Air Force)*

Adequate air defense

If one realises that just four minutes after taking-off from an East German air base near Berlin a super-fast MiG-25 can be flying over cities such as Hanover and Hamburg, it becomes obvious that a short reaction time is vital for adequate air defense. For the air defense of the Central Sector which, roughly, covers the area Denmark, the Benelux and the Federal Republic of Germany, NATO has, therefore, opted for a strict form of organization known as the Central Region's Integrated Air Defense System (IADS). In IADS all the air defence units of Belgium, the FRG, Canada, Great Britain, the Netherlands and the US are integrated; the interceptor squadrons, the surface-to-air missiles (SAMs) and the radar systems of the NADGE radar network (NATO Air Defense Ground Environment) that stretches from the North Pole to Turkey. The Boeing E-3A Sentry aircraft of the NATO Early Warning System add a considerable contribution because the powerful radars of these flying radar stations have a range of more than 400 kilometers. An E-3A cruising over the FRG at a height of around 40,000 feet can, therefore, see over the horizon as far as Warsaw and beyond Budapest and warn of hostile attacks in good time. The F-15C Eagles of the 36th TFW at Bitburg and the 32nd TFS were stationed at Soesterberg in the Netherlands (the 32nd switched to the Eagle in 1978) and also an element of the IADS. In total the USAFE now has more than a hundred F-15s stationed in Europe; a considerable reinforcement of NATO's air defense in the vulnerable Central Sector.

'Zulu Alert'

The two F-15C units come under the 4th Allied Tactical Air Force of NATO. This Allied air force is responsible for the air defense of the Central Sector and can also be used in the north of the FRG, the Benelux and parts of the North Sea and Denmark.

Above: Several F-4E Phantoms went to the newly-formed 313rd TFS at Hahn Air Base, Germany. *(Cees Steijger)*

Overleaf: The McDonnell Douglas F-15 Eagle was designed for air superiority. Here two Netherlands-based Eagles show their muscles. *(McDonnell Douglas)*

As a rule, a number of fighters are kept ready for immediate operation at the 4th ATAF's airfields, or as the jargon puts it, kept at Quick Reaction Alert (QRA). In addition, a number of fully armed F-15Cs at both airfields are also kept ready to start in a so-called 'Zulu Alert' hangar near the runway strip. They are always loaded with four AIM-7F Sparrow radar-guided missiles of four AIM-120A AMRAAMs (Advanced Medium Range Air-to-Air Missiles) and four heat-seeking AIM-9M Sidewinders and around 900 20 mm shells for the General Electric six-barrel rotary cannon. Within a few minutes of a 'Scramble' the QRA F-15C's can be 'up and at 'em'.

Although most scrambles are training exercises, the NATO commanders in their underground Control and Reporting Centres (CRSs) do, quite often, sound the alarm for an Alpha Scramble. Alpha Scrambles generally involve the interception of unidentified aircraft or civil airliners flying — for whatever reason — over forbidden military areas. These lost aircraft are called Zombies and are very often deliberately off-course Eastern European civil aircraft that have all too willingly come to take a peep at NATO's military bases. The F-15s seldom intercept Eastern Bloc aircraft yet, according to the American aviation writer Michael Skinner, there was talk of border violations along the border between the FRG and GDR involving East European combat aircraft. Although such violations

were often of short duration, the Bitburg F-15s were still despatched on an Alpha scramble to the Air Defense Identification Zone (ADIZ) along the Eastern Bloc border. In this fifty kilometers-wide air defense zone all aircraft are carefully identified as 'friend or foe' by NATO's Sector Operations Centres.

The F-15's avionics are fully tuned to air defense. The aircraft has an extremely sensitive Hughes APG-63 radar that can register aircraft 160 kilometers away and select them for the fire control computer. This means hostile aircraft can be attacked with air-to-air missiles without any warning when they are still ninety kilometers away and wherever they are in the sky; the Hughes radar is a lookdown-shootdown type which can find both low and high flying aircraft.

Despite excellent performance and advanced avionics, intercepting an intruder in time is not a simple matter. Which is why there were always armed F-15Cs in the air patrolling the ADIZ. The Combat Air Patrol (CAP) missions generally involve two to four aircraft which rendezvous with Boeing KC-135 tankers from the European Tanker Task Force during the mission to enable them to stay in the air for hours at a time.

Above: Northrop F-5E Tiger II number '34' of the 527th TFTAS in 1977. *(Collection Cees Steijger)*

Top: Close formation flying of three Bitburg F-15s.
(McDonnell Douglas)

In response to the siting of SS-20s the United States stationed four squadrons (about ninety aircraft) of F-111Fs at RAF Lakenheath in Suffolk. This involved some extensive and complicated shuffling of units, which was carried out under the project name 'Ready Switch'. The 48th TFW at Lakenheath transferred its F-4D Phantoms to the 388th TFW at Hill AFB and the 474th TFW at Nellis, in exchange for F-111Fs from the 366th TFW at Mountain Home, New Mexico. The 474th TFW gave its older F-111As to the 366th TFW and received further F-4D Phantoms from the 49th TFW at Holloman AFB, New Mexico. Not surprisingly, Ready Switch took almost a year to complete.

The Pentagon wanted an F-111E/F Strike Force in Europe that would form the core of a nuclear force in NATO. Details were published in *Aviation Week & Space Technology* on 7 July 1980. All F-111E/F aircraft were to be fitted with Pave Tack equipment that would enable them to launch small tactical nuclear missiles day and night and in all types of weather. The Pave Tack system used the latest laser technology to facilitate precision bombing. Briefly, a laser beam aimed at the target served as a 'flight path' for both conventional and nuclear Pave Way bombs.

The F-111E and F-111F remain the USAF's most advanced tactical bomber in Europe. Both are equipped with a Texas Instruments APQ-119 advanced navigation and attack radar as well as a very accurate terrain-following radar, and thus equipped have been the USAF's only aircraft to be able to penetrate enemy airspace almost unhindered until the advent of the Stealth machines such as the Northrop B-2.

★   ★   ★

It's green and it flies

According to NATO estimates, at the end of the 1970s the combined Warsaw Pact armies could field around 40,000 tanks compared to NATO's some 15,000. NATO also lagged far behind in numbers of launching installations for anti-tank weapons, the 'score' being Warsaw Pact 24,000; NATO 9,300. This uncomfortable situation had been acknowledged for many years and provided the impulse for the development of an aircraft specifically designed to combat tanks.

During the Vietnam War, hundreds of Bell UH-1 helicopters equipped with machine-guns were used to attack tanks and vehicles. Later, Douglas A-1 Skyraiders were used and the USAF even went so far as to fit C-130 Hercules transports with 105 mm howitzers. In the unequal fight these C-130 Gunships were the most effective. As a result of experience gained with anti-tank aircraft in Vietnam, the Fairchild A-10 Thunderbolt II was designed. This aircraft is fitted with twin turbofans and can loiter over a target and fire a six meter-long seven-barrelled 30 mm General Electric rotary cannon with a firing rate of more than 4,000 rounds per minute.

With its two engines mounted one on each side of the fuselage, its flat slab of a wing that almost sits under the aircraft and the two stubby tail fins, it is little wonder that pilots refer to it as the Warthog. When it comes to close air support (CAS) of ground troops it performs magnificently and is a tank-killer par excellence. The aircraft can also carry up to 8,000 kg of weapons (which is around 1,000 kg more than the F-4) including AGM-65 Maverick TV-camera guided air-to-ground missiles.

CAS missions are vulnerable to ground fire, so most of the underside of the aircraft is made of armoured titanium. The hog drivers as the A-70 pilots are affectionately known are protected by a titanium 'bathtub' capable of withstanding direct hits from the ground. In addition, the fuel tanks have an explosion-resistant foam layer that prevents the tanks bursting into flame after a direct hit. The aircraft is so designed that even at extremely low speeds and low altitude it has magnificent manoeuvrability. To stay out of reach of hostile radar the A-10 generally flies at nearly ground level during CAS missions.

Its camouflage scheme is called 'Europe 1' by the Americans and was specially designed for European conditions. The American aviation writer Michael Skinner wrote in *USAFE: the primer of modern air combat in Europe* that the colours used by the A-10 are made from a special type of paint that can absorb sixty per cent of the sun's rays. Because different densities of

A formation of two fully-armed F-15C Eagles on combat air patrol over Germany. *(McDonnell Douglas)*

paint are used its colours change in different light conditions, giving a sort of chameleon effect.

The USAFE has had around 120 A-10 Thunderbolt IIs since 1978. Originally all the aircraft belonged to the 81st TFW stationed, with six squadrons, at the twin Bentwaters/Woodbridge air bases. Later two squadrons moved to the 10th TFW at Alconbury. A-10 detachments are also stationed continuously at four Forward Operating Locations (FOLs) in the FRG at Nörvenich and Alhorn (2nd ATAF) and at Sembach and Leipheim (4th ATAF). Rotating between their main operating bases in England and these forward bases ensures the A-10 pilots become familiar with flying conditions in Germany.

Despite its talents as a tank killer, the A-10 is handicapped during the CAS missions by its limited 550 km/h speed, particularly now air defense is becoming more and more sophisticated and mobile defense missiles can be fired from shoulder carried launchers. In practice this means that to prevent the air defense systems' computers time to lock-on to the aircraft, which could have unfortunate consequences, an A-10 never flies in the same direction for more than a few seconds at a time.

★　★　★

Top: A-10s at Bentwaters in 1978. *(Henk Koerts)*

Above: Coronet Mill in 1978: Twelve F-4C Phantoms of the 93rd TFS of the AFRes at Homestead, Florida, went to Sola Air Base in Norway. *(Collection Cees Steijger)*

'Coronet' for fast reinforcement

In the second half of the 1970s, the fast reinforcement of NATO in times of crisis as an element of the Flexible Rapid Response doctrine was given a positive push with the introduction of so-called 'Coronet' deployments. This type of deployment generally entails units of the Air National Guard being posted to NATO bases for several weeks and takes place within the framework of the 'Total Force' concept. Although this concept was firmly formed in 1973, its implementation as far as reinforcement of Europe was concerned was delayed several years by the Vietnam War.

The basic idea behind this new concept was that units of the Air National Guard (ANG) and the Air Force Reserve (AFRes) should be capable of mobilizing quickly and then operating as active USAF units. This, obviously, requires the American National Reserve squadrons being trained, which is one reason the Coronet deployments were introduced. They both test the rapid reinforcement of NATO and give the ANG and AFRes squadrons, and indeed the TAC squadrons, an opportunity to gain flying experience in Europe.

If the deployment is large-scale involving tens of aircraft and hundreds of personnel, information as to when and where it is going is generally released several months beforehand. But Coronet deployments can also come as a complete surprise to the squadron involved. Exactly how many deployments are planned for a given year is, therefore, kept very quiet and can vary between twenty to fifty ranging from small deployments for just a short while, to large scale deployments involving multiple squadrons of A-7 Corsairs, for example.

In 1976, as an extension to the new Coronet deployments, the AAFCE nominate certain airfields as Collocated Operating Bases (COBs). These airfields were equipped to accommodate any Coronet deployment at any moment. According to the respected NATO journal *NATO's Sixteen Nations*, there are now more than fifty COBs spread over the whole of Western Europe. By far the most can be found in the FRG and England, which have around twenty each. But there are also COBs in countries such as Turkey, Greece, the Netherlands, Denmark and in Norway, where eight of the Norwegian Air Force's fourteen airfields are designated as COBs. As far as is known the first Coronet deployment was sent to Norway in

February 1978 when seventeen RF-4C reconnaissance aircraft from three ANG squadrons departed for the Norwegian Sola airfield near Stavanger. This deployment was code-named 'Coronet Snipe' and lasted almost a month.

Another important deployment took place at the end of August 1978 when eight F-111Ds from the 27th TFW at Cannon AFB, New Mexico, were sent to Gardermoer air base just outside Oslo. This deployment (codename 'Coronet Kingfisher') formed part of NATO's regular 'Northern Wedding' which is primarily a naval exercise aimed at testing the defense of the vulnerable Atlantic supply routes.

According to the *Mach Meter*, the 27th TFW's base newspaper, for a period of four weeks the F-111Ds carried out sea surveillance and anti-ship warfare (ASW) missions, primarily over the vital supply routes in the North Sea and the Atlantic Ocean between Norway and Iceland. One hundred and twenty missions were flown from Gardermoer during which the F-111Ds carried out simulated attacks on 'enemy' ships with anti-ship missiles.

A cold fight

Defending the Atlantic supply lines has always been a sore point for NATO. Norway, that should play a significant part in the defense, is forced more and more to lean on the alliance. For many years the Norwegians have had to contend with considerable financial problems. The acquisition of 72 General Dynamics F-16As in the 1970s was a heavy burden for their defense budget. Too heavy, in fact; in the period 1979-1983 defense modernization lagged seriously behind. In an article published in the Norwegian magazine *Norsk*

Top: The F-4Ds from the 48th TFW at Lakenheath, England, were replaced by F-111Fs in 1976. *(Cees Steijger)*

Above: Many DACT-exercises are conducted at Decimomannu Air Base, Sardinia. *(Cees Steijger)*

Militaert Tidsskrift in July 1985, a researcher from the Norwegian Defense Research Establishment, Ragnvald Solstrand, revealed that in monetary terms the scope of the lag in 1985 equalled the total value of the Norwegian Navy's equipment at that moment; around fifteen billion Krone. Moreover, the Norwegian air force, like almost every other NATO air force, must contend with a crippling shortage of fighter pilots. In 1985 there were only 43 pilots, including instructors, for the remaining fleet of 68 F-16s.

Above: Russian MiG-23 Floggers . . . USAFE imitated them. *(Collection Cees Steijger)*

Top: A silver F-5E Tiger shortly before a DACT-mission from Alconbury. *(Henk Koerts)*

Right: The 32nd TFS at Soesterberg, the Netherlands, switched to F-15 Eagles in 1978. *(McDonnell Douglas)*

Clearly the 'Norwegian Balance' is out of kilter and this means that one way and the other the security of this strategically vital area of NATO depends on the Alliance. The facilities available to support the Norwegians include the ACE Mobile Forces — a mobile NATO strike force established in 1961 — the Canadian Air Sea Transportable Brigade, the UK/NL Landing Force (United Kingdom and the Netherlands navies) and American, British and Canadian (CAF) Canadian Armed Forces' squadrons. This support is vitally important not only for the defense of the Norwegian borders, particularly the border with the Soviet Union, but also for the defense of the sea routes that are indispensable for the reinforcement of NATO from America.

According to NATO strategy a conflict between the Warsaw Pact and NATO will be fought out first in central Europe and reserve troops, supplies, etc, will be transported immediately from Canada and the US to Europe both via air and the Atlantic Ocean. It may be assumed that the Soviet Navy in particular will do everything possible to disrupt, or even blockade, NATO's shipping routes. The Soviet Navy can attack

the supply lines from the Black Sea, the Baltic or from the large marine bases at Murmansk at the northernmost point of the Kola Peninsula. Attacks from the Black Sea or the Baltic must always pass the Bosphorus or the Skagerak, respectively, both of which are controlled by NATO. Whatever happens the fight will certainly be centred around the 'sea-gate' bordered by Greenland, Iceland and Norway. For this reason NATO needs a strong Norwegian defense, which is why the USAF sends several Coronet deployments to the Norwegian airfields along the Atlantic coast every year.

During the past few years this has generally entailed USAF squadrons from the ANG. The American Navy and Marine Corps have also gradually become involved in Norway's defense, obviously because these units are more directed towards anti-ship warfare than the USAF.

Atlantic defense

In peacetime a large portion of the area in which the Atlantic shipping lanes lie is guarded by Boeing E-3A AWACS (Airborne Warning and Control System). Two of these flying radar stations are stationed permanently at Keflavik air base near Reykjavik, Iceland, along with a squadron of F-15 interceptors. These aircraft form part of the Iceland Defense Force, a strike force established in 1951, at the request of the Icelandic government, to defend the island and its surrounding seas. While it is true that Iceland has been a member of NATO since 1949, it has no military force of its own as this is hardly a viable proposition for an island with a population of less than 250,000.

The defense agreement between Iceland and the US in which it is stated that 'the US, on behalf of the North Atlantic Treaty Organization, will take all measures for the defense of Iceland' dates from 1951. And it is very necessary because, thanks to its geographical location, halfway between New York and Moscow, the island is of vital strategic importance. It also lies in the middle of the so-called GIN-gap — the ocean between Greenland, Iceland and Norway. This GIN-gap is particularly important for the Soviet Union both because it gives access to the Atlantic and the North Sea and because it contains NATO's vital shipping lanes.

There is not only extensive Russian naval activity in this area, the Russian air force is also well represented and frequently spurs the air defense in the Icelandic Military Defense Identification Zone (MADIZ), that stretched 320 kilometers out from the coast, into action. The interceptions are not the responsibility of the USAFE but rather of the TAC's 57th Fighter Interceptor Squadron.

Above: In the sixties the 57th FIS was equipped with Convair F-102 Delta Dagger interceptors. *(DoD)*

Top: Intercepting a Soviet Tu-95 Bear over the Atlantic are two F-15Cs from the US Air Force's 57th FIS at Keflavik Air Base. *(US Air Force)*

In the 1950s the then Aerospace Defense Command was charged with the air defense of the region and for a long time used Northrop F-89 Scorpion interceptor-fighters. Later these aircraft were replaced by Convair F-102 Delta Daggers which in their turn made way for McDonnell Douglas F-4C and F-4E Phantoms (at the end of 1985 the 57th FIS was equipped with McDonnell Douglas F-15C Eagles). The object of 95 per cent of scrambles from Keflavik is the identification and shadowing of Soviet aircraft in the MADIZ.

Since 1963 the 57th FIS has intercepted over 2,000 Soviet aircraft and the present average is around 150 per year. The majority of aircraft intercepted originate from Murmansk and are usually Tupolev Tu-95 Bears en route to Cuba. But during NATO sea exercises, such as 'Northern Wedding', Tupolev Tu-16 Badgers and Ilyushin IL-18 Coots are also frequently intercepted. All aircraft movements are monitored by the Boeing E-3A AWACS of the 552nd Airborne Warning and Control Wing — a detachment from Tinker AFB, Oklahoma.

The American air force also operates two large radar stations on Iceland; one several kilometers north of Reykjavik and the other near Hofn in the south-east. Both stations form part of the North American Aerospace Defense Command (NORAD) which registers every aircraft movement as far as the Arctic Circle. Tu-95 Bears from the Kola Peninsula are often observed cruising along the Norwegian coast where they are promptly intercepted by Norwegian fighters. If they continue flying south, they find English interceptors from Leuchars airfield in Scotland waiting for them.

Every once in a while the Bears sneak along at low altitude to stay off NATO's radar screens in Norway and Iceland. They then suddenly pop up in the middle of the MADIZ causing the interceptors from Keflavik to scramble. While most interceptions are mere routine jobs that take place without incident, there are times when a hint of aggression creeps in. One such occurred when a — perhaps nervous — crew of a Coot tossed out sonar buoys and dragged tens of meters of antenna cable to thwart the interceptors. Although the exception rather than the rule, this incident is one of the cat-and-mouse games played between East and West in this part of the Atlantic.

Chapter 8
Into the eighties and onwards

The 1970s ended with the star of modernization still shining brightly over the USAFE. Hardly was the 32nd Tactical Fighter Squadron at Soesterberg air base, the Netherlands, declared operational with its new F-15A Eagles when the aircraft were replaced by improved F-15Cs. And several Phantom wings switched to General Dynamics F-16A Fighting Falcons. But more sweeping changes were imminent as the American Congress made funds available for an expansion of the air force in Europe. The A-10 combat group at Bentwaters/Woodbridge was expanded with two additional squadrons. A European Tankers Task Force was established at Fairford air base in England. The 11th Strategic Group, also at Fairford, was equipped with fifteen Boeing KC-135A Stratotankers for use during deployments and exercises. And the stationing in England of one squadron of the latest Lockheed TR-1 high-altitude reconnaissance aircraft plus a squadron with advanced EF-111A Raven flying jammers was on the cards. This modernisation and expansion occurred at a time when international political developments were taking place that would shape events until well into the 1980s.

SS-20s pointing at Europe

The mobile SS-20 nuclear surface-to-surface missile was a stumbling block in East-West relations. Hundreds were pointed at European targets from launching sites in East Germany. According to the International Institute for Strategic Studies in London, by 1975 the US had lost its strategic nuclear lead over the Soviet Union and with the introduction of the SS-20 had even fallen behind. NATO's answer was not long in coming and on 12 December 1979 NATO decided to deploy 572 new nuclear missiles in Europe: 108 Pershing 2 Missiles and 464 cruise missiles. Of the cruise missiles, 160 were stationed in England, 96 in the Federal Republic, 112 in Italy, 48 in the Netherlands and 48 in Belgium. All 108 Pershings were stationed in the Federal Republic.

The second significant aspect of the NATO decision was the readiness to 'horse trade' with the Soviet Union for the reduction or total elimination of these missiles against similar reductions or elimination of the Russian SS-20s. East-West relations were put under more pressure by the Soviet troops' invasion of Afghanistan during the Christmas holiday of 1979. Together the Soviet troops and Afghan government troops took up the fight against Islamic rebels. In his reaction to this brutal assault, Jimmy Carter, the then American President, said that, under the circumstances, ratification of the new SALT-2 Agreement — the agreement between the US and the Soviet Union concerning the maximum number of strategic nuclear missiles on both sides — would be improper. The American Congress agreed wholeheartedly.

American embassy under fire

Indignant reaction to the Soviet invasion came from other countries around the world, including Iran where furious adherents of the Islamic revolution stormed the Soviet Embassy in Teheran. Turbulent Teheran was the centre of Islamic revolution and the backdrop for almost daily pro-Islamic mass demonstrations.

The American embassy in Teheran had also recently come under fire from armed Iranian students, but for a totally different reason. It happened on 4 November 1979. The students overran the Embassy and took all the staff on site hostage. The followers of spiritual leader Khomeni accused the American embassy personnel of espionage and said they would not be released until Shah Reza Pahlavi, who had fled to the US, was returned.

President Carter refused to surrender the Shah which hindered all further attempts to free the American hostages. Carter could do nothing more than take retaliatory measures. Arms deliveries to Iran were halted, Iranian assets in American banks were frozen, oil imports were stopped and Iranian students in the US were deported. The President had few other options, apart from freeing the staff in the embassy by force, and so, on the advice of his Security Adviser Zbigniew Brzezinski, this is what he decided to do. The daring operation, which involved both the Marines and the Air Force, including units of the USAFE stationed in Europe, failed tragically and cost eight American lives.

Above: A General Dynamics F-16C of the USAFE's 86th Air Division at Ramstein Air Base, FRG. *(General Dynamics)*

Opposite: The big Sikorsky RH-53D helicopter was chosen for the risky operation in Iran. *(Sikorsky)*

Discreet preparations

Very soon after the hostages were taken in Iran, planning of the rescue operation began in the deepest secrecy. Marine Corps helicopter pilots and specialists were recruited and training began in January 1980 under the leadership of Charles Beckwith. Beckwith was the US Army Colonel in charge of Operational Detachment Delta — an army unit established on the same lines as the Israeli and West German units that had carried out successful rescue operations at Entebbe and Mogadishu.

The Iranian operation used special versions of both the Lockheed C-130 Hercules and the large Sikorsky RH-53D Sea Stallion helicopter. The RH-53D was chosen because of its range — a large portion of the operation would be carried out over Iranian territory. Secrecy also played a role and unarmed RH-53Ds from minesweeper units on board aircraft carriers would be unobtrusive and never be suspected of being involved in an illegal operation. Six of these helicopters were ferried in massive Lockheed C-5A Galaxy transports to the American support post on Diego Garcia island in the Indian Ocean from where the machines were flown first to the aircraft carrier USS *Kitty Hawk* and then in January 1980 to the USS *Nimitz* which had, meanwhile, arrived in the operation zone. For the operation the twenty-ton Sea Stallions were fitted with advanced navigation equipment and optical night vision systems in case night flying was required. The minesweeping equipment was taken out to make room for additional fuel tanks which added several hundreds of kilometers of range.

Sadat knew?

The CIA had good, detailed maps of the area — the region had been well surveyed during the 1970s as part of an earthquake research programme. During the survey an airstrip lying on the Tabas-Yazd road near Posht-e-Badam, around 500 kilometers south of Teheran, was used. In the rescue plan this airstrip was designated Desert One; another landing area nearer Teheran was designated Desert Two.

The two airstrips which, in fact, were little more than flat areas of sand, were checked for their suitability weeks before the operation. The reconnaissance flights over Iranian territory were probably made by Lockheed C-130E Hercules transports which, like the Iranian air force's own C-130s, were painted in a sand coloured camouflage scheme. As early as January 1980 sand coloured C-130s were observed at Nellis AFB in Nevada. It may be assumed that the rescue operation was rehearsed in the desert around Nellis.

On 9 April 1980, aircraft spotters at Mildenhall air base, Suffolk, where the American 3rd Air Force is headquartered, saw a C-130 in desert camouflage take off for Cairo-West airfield in Egypt. During the preparatory phase a SAC U-2R was also detached to the American support post on Diego Garcia. According to an article about the U-2R/TR-1 in *Air International*, this U-2R was almost certainly used for spy flights over Iran. A remarkable adjunct is that on 7 April President Anwar Sadat of Egypt broke his journey to Washington to make a short visit to Mildenhall. Considering the fact that Cairo-West airfield played a role both before and after the operation, it is probable that Sadat's visit to Mildenhall has something to do with the rescue operation and it is even possible that Sadat was party to the American plans.

Charred bodies and wreckage of a C-130 and a helicopter lie in the desert near the Posht-e-Badam oasis following the failure of the US mission to rescue the American hostages in Teheran. *(ANP)*

On 22 April 1980, two days before the rescue attempt, eight C-130 transports arrived at Cairo-West having crossed the Atlantic in two formations. They were refuelled over the Azores by Boeing KC-135 Stratotankers from Mildenhall. The transports were special MC-130E and EC-130E Hercules from the 8th Special Operations Squadron at Hulburt Field AFB, Florida and the 7th Airborne Command & Control Squadron from Keesler AFB, Mississippi.

Drama in the desert

At half past seven on the morning of 24 April, eight RH-53D helicopters took-off from USS *Nimitz* somewhere in the Persian Gulf and set course for Desert One where six C-130s were waiting to refuel them. Flying at an average altitude of thirty meters, the aircraft remained out of the reach of Iranian radar and penetrated Iranian airspace undetected.

Problems arose before they were even a third of the way to Desert One. Crossing an extensive dusty region, in which the pilots' vision was restricted to just a few meters, the RH-53s almost lost their way and one helicopter developed a technical problem with the rotor blades and had to be left behind in the desert while the crew transferred to another machine. Soon after, a second RH-53 was in trouble and the pilot decided to return to the USS *Nimitz*. Now there were six RH-53s. They arrived at Desert One between one and one and a half hours late. The C-130s carrying the combat teams, the weapons and ammunition and a large quantity of fuel for the helicopters had been waiting for two hours, with engines running the whole time to avoid any problems with take-off.

While the RH-53s were being refuelled a serious defect was discovered in the hydraulic system of one of the helicopters. The defect was too serious to allow the helicopter to fly on. Now there were five RH-53s, too few, it was considered, to carry out the operation successfully. Operations Command on board the *Nimitz* was consulted and, in turn, Washington. When the situation was explained to him, President Carter cancelled the entire operation.

At that moment all the helicopters had enough fuel to begin the return flight apart from one which was only partially refuelled and had to fly to another of the C-130s for the tanks to be completely filled. This C-130 had just finished refuelling another of the RH-53s which prepared to make room for its colleague. The manoeuvre had dramatic results. Perhaps partially blinded by the enormous cloud of dust thrown up by the rotor blades, the helicopter pilot collided with the C-130's left wing. The two machines burst into flames and, because the C-130 was full of ammunition the situation was hopeless; in the sea of fire eight crew lost their lives. A daring rescue attempt had turned into a deadly failure.

The European connection

The USAFE's involvement during the Iranian affair was patently obvious. First, there was President Sadat's visit to the 3rd Air Force's headquarters at Mildenhall. The original destination of the Presidential Boeing 707 was Lajes but, according to the official version, there were reports of Libyan terrorists in the area and it was feared the Boeing would be shot down. But choosing Mildenhall as detour airfield was in no way 'purely coincidental'.

Boeing KC-135A of the European Tanker Task Force taking off from Fairford. Note that this KC-135 is equipped with the probe and drogue refuelling system, which is only occasionally used by the USAF. *(Collection Cees Steijger)*

Several weeks before the Iranian rescue operation, aircraft later used in the action were at this military air base. First, three C-130s in special desert camouflage were seen. Then on 19 April five KC-135A tankers from the 305th ARW at Grissom AFB, Indiana, were observed. Of itself, not remarkable at this air base where KC-135s land and take-off several times a day. But the 305th ARW's tankers are not ordinary aircraft and are rarely seen, even at Mildenhall. Four of the 305th ARW's tankers are converted EC-135 Airborne Command Posts — with most of the electronics still on board — that can themselves be refuelled in the air. The fifth is a converted RC-135D (serial number *00362*) electronic reconnaissance aircraft that flew for a long time with the 55th Strategic Reconnaissance Wing at Offutt AFB, Nebraska. Soon after they landed at Mildenhall, the five special KC-135s took off again for Cairo-West airfield in Egypt. Although there is no real proof it is highly probably that these tankers were used to refuel the C-130s taking part in the rescue operation (over Saudi Arabia?).

According to the British journalist E. P. Thompson there were far more activities related to the Iranian rescue operation going on in England. In an article about nuclear armament published in May 1980 in the *New Left Review*, Thompson wrote that shortly before the Iranian operation, the Pentagon brought the F-111Fs of the 48th Tactical Fighter Wing at Lakenheath to a state of readiness. Whether or not the Pentagon was actually planning a surprise attack on Teheran is not known. Equally unclear is whether the three Boeing B-52D Stratofortress bombers which arrived at RAF Marham the day before the Iranian operation (by chance?) were in any way involved.

KC-135s at Fairford

As the number of deployments to European air bases increased and European airspace became very busy, particularly during the traditional NATO autumn exercise, the USAFE's need for its own tanker unit grew. The decision to form a European Tanker Task Force (ETTF) in Europe was taken by Air Force Command in Washington at the end of 1977. Initially the plan was to station fifteen ETTF KC-135s at Greenham Common, but the local residents protested mightily and managed to torpedo the posting on the grounds of noise. In June 1978, after an evaluation of eighteen English airfields, the British Parliament decided the heavy tankers should go to Fairford in the west of England and this is where the 11th Strategic Group was established. In September 1979, when the necessary preparations were complete, the first five KC-135s arrived. A year later another five arrived and in March 1981 the full strength of fifteen tankers was reached. The European KC-135s were involved in 'Coronet' and 'Crested Cap' deployments to and from Europe but perhaps their most vital task was aerial refuelling of USAFE and NATO combat aircraft.

Refuelling in time of crisis — a precarious business

NATO's airfields all lie within range of the Warsaw Pact's surface-to-surface missiles and it may be assumed that NATO's infrastructure would be among the Warsaw Pact's primary targets if it ever came to hostilities. The airfields would certainly be on the 'hit list', not perhaps for attack with nuclear SS-20s or similar weapons but rather with airfield denial weapons. In any event, the most important airfields would be unusable for some time.

Above: F-16A of the Multinational Operational Test and Evaluation team (MOT&E) photographed at Leeuwarden Air Base, the Netherlands, in August 1980. *(Cees Steijger)*

Top: C-130E (serial number 39810) wearing desert camouflage was seen passing through Mildenhall in early March 1980. The day after the ill-fated mission in Iran the same aircraft was spotted at Ramstein Air Base, FRG. *(Collection Cees Steijger)*

In World War 2 the fighters could take off and land on improvised landing fields if they had to. Today's fighters can land only on hard surfaces. If the runways at their home base are damaged they must find an alternative — intact — base at which to land. Such bases will be far from the battlefield and fuel will become a problem. The fighters will need to refuel in the air.

In an article published in NATO's authoritative journal *NATO's Sixteen Nations* at the end of 1983, Mark Berents, a former American fighter pilot, cast doubt on the tactical possibilities of refuelling in the air under war conditions. First of all, the great tactical radius of the Soviet Union's latest fighters such as the MiG-29 Fulcrum and the Sukhoi Su-27 Flanker brings France and the British Isles within reach without the need to refuel. The USAFE tankers fleet would be forced to operate from the west of England and France or even the Mediterranean region. Add to that the fact that a MiG pilot does not even need to be within sight of a refuelling operation but can fire an air-to-air missile, such as the AA-6 Acrid, in the direction of a tanker from up to ninety kilometers away and it becomes obvious just how precarious aerial refuelling in war conditions can be.

Berents, who gained a great deal of experience as a fighter pilot in Vietnam, points out that a missile attack on a refuelling operation causes panic and confusion among the pilots with the resulting danger of kerosene spillage and collision. According to Berents, just hearing 'MiiiiiiiGs . . !' over the radio is enough to cause total chaos.

But the fighters must be able to fly to and from the battle zone, which is why refuelling in the air has become such an important element in USAFE's total training programme. During the training missions the combat aircraft often 'hook-up' with one of the KC-135s from ETTF's fleet at Fairford. Belgian, Danish, Dutch and Norwegian air forces also train regularly with the American KC-135s. NATO F-16s that, for example, participate in exercises in the United States, are generally refuelled by American KC-135s over the Atlantic.

F-16, the latest fighter

At the beginning of 1974, the year in which the brand new McDonnell Douglas F-15 Eagle was taken into service with TAC, the first test flights were made with the YF-16. This relatively small combat aircraft was General Dynamics' trump card in the USAF's lightweight fighter programme. This programme, in which Northrop also participated with the YF-17, was aimed at developing a replacement for the McDonnell Douglas F-4 Phantom. After lengthy evaluation the USAF finally opted for the YF-16 and in 1975 placed an initial

order for 650 aircraft. Supplementary orders for 738 aircraft and 720 aircraft were placed in 1977 and 1986 respectively.

F-4Es of the 50th TFW landing at Hahn. In 1981 Hahn was home of the first USAFE F-16s. *(Cees Steijger)*

The F-16 was designed around the Pratt & Whitney F-100 turbofan, the power source used in the F-15, which delivers a maximum thrust of over 11,000 kg. By using modern non-metallic composite materials such as graphite and carbon, the F-16's take-off weight was reduced by just over 10,000 kg resulting in a 1.1:1 thrust/weight ratio — which means the thrust delivered by the engines is greater than the weight of the aircraft. The F-16 also has excellent aerodynamics — its short stubby winged flow under the cockpit and wings and fuselage blend together. Combined, the F-16's thrust/weight ratio and aerodynamics add up to phenomenal performance and extreme manoeuvrability, particularly at subsonic speeds. These characteristics really come into their own during air combat because in a dog fight victory often depends on fast acceleration and manoeuvrability and the F-16's allow it to perform extreme manoeuvres pulling up to 9G.

As even an experienced pilot can only handle these excessive speeds for a few seconds at a time, the F-16 incorporates features which protect the pilot from the ill effects of high G-forces such as black-outs. The ejector seat is tilted 30° back; an extremely comfortable position for the pilot and one which gives a 1G advantage. And rather than a conventional joy-stick the F-16 has a so-called 'side stick' very similar to the control stick on a home computer. The tiny side stick hardly moves but measures the force applied by the pilot's hand. Pressing the side stick in a particular direction sends electronic signals to the Lear Siegler flight control computer which calculates the correct flap and rudder settings and transmits them to the relevant steering and hydraulic systems. This is why the system is known as a fly-by-wire control system.

With many superlatives the trade press hailed the F-16 as the pinnacle of fighter perfection. The aircraft can be used for both air-to-air combat supporting air defense and as a tactical strike aircraft for air-to-surface attack. For an air combat mission the F-16 is usually armed with two heat-seeking AIM-9L Sidewinder missiles — a maximum of six can be carried — in addition to its standard 20 mm Vulcan rotary cannon with a firing rate of 6,000 rounds per minute. The aircraft has nine external weapons stations, two wingtip, six underwing and one fuselage, which can carry a wide variety of stores including conventional bombs, ECM equipment, TV-guided AGM-65D Maverick missiles and laser-guided weapons and the F-16C can carry this ordinance load over a long distance; its combat radius is more than 800 kilometers. This vastly improved version of the F-16 is a so-called all weather fighter and of all the USAF's aircraft only the General Dynamics F-111 can surpass its blind-bombing accuracy in bad weather or at twilight.

★　　★　　★

149

Above: Tomahawk cruise missile is launched from a transporter-erector-launcher (TEL). *(DoD)*

Opposite: A specially-designed remote-controlled hydraulic trailer is used to load Air Launch Cruise Missiles (ALCM) onto the pylon of a B52 Stratofortress aircraft from the 92nd bombing wing. *(US Air Force)*

In March 1981 the British government gave permission for the USAFE to station a tactical reconnaissance squadron of Lockheed TR-1A spy planes at Alconbury. Originally, eighteen of these high altitude reconnaissance aircraft were to be stationed at Alconbury, but by 1990 the squadron comprised only twelve aircraft. Although the 95th Reconnaissance Squadron, which operates the TR-1As, is an SAC squadron it is under the USAFE's command. The Alconbury TR-1As are also used for SIGINT and photo-reconnaissance missions. Besides that, and this is the main difference between the U-2R and the TR-1A, the TR-1A can be fitted with ASARS-2 radar (Advanced Synthetic Aperture Radar System) — an extremely accurate sideways looking radar — and the advanced PLSS system.

To way behind the Iron Curtain

According to articles in *Aviation Week & Space Technology*, a TR-1A with an ASAR-2 radar flying at around 65,000 feet, 48 kilometers from the front line (Forward Edge of the Battle Area — FEBA), can see eighty kilometers into enemy territory. The ASAR-2 radar can also produce pictures with an almost photographic quality on which tank formations, mobile command posts, etc, show up crystal clear. Most important, these pictures can be transmitted in real-time, via secret data-links, to Central Processing Stations (CPS) on the ground where the information can be evaluated and passed on to troops in the field so they can, for example, prepare for an attack before the enemy tanks have even reached the battle zone.

The Precision Locator Strike System goes a step further. The information gathered by the system is transmitted to either a ground station or a flying Boeing E-3A AWACS (Airborne Warning and Control System) from where fighters are directed to the located targets.

Fire-and-forget weapons can be launched by the fighter pilots from a safe distance and left to find their targets by themselves using the PLSS information. A PLSS mission involves three TR-1As at a time that follow a so-called racetrack course along the frontline. When an enemy radar signal is detected the time at which it is received by each of the TR-1As is registered and passed on to the CPS or AWACS aircraft (time of arrival technique). Through a complicated triangulation the target's exact location can be calculated and the co-ordinates transmitted to the fighters.

According to American military authorities, the system is very reliable and even functions perfectly after the enemy radar station has been shut down to avoid detection; just one pulse is all that is needed to make an accurate position calculation. Details of the PLSS system's performance have not been officially released but because the TR-1A operates above 65,000 feet it is assumed it has a range of 300 kilometers. This means that a TR-1A can see far into Eastern Europe from NATO airspace. From racetracks along their borders, large tracts of the Eastern European countries can be covered, while from the Baltic much of Russia is within range.

'Wild Weasels' take on radar

NATO reports suggest that the Warsaw Pact's air defense is extremely well developed and has, for many years, been built around mobile SAM batteries (Surface-to-Air Missiles) and radar-guided anti-aircraft artillery. The wars in the Middle East and Vietnam have taught that these relatively simple defense weapons are capable of bringing down the most advanced aircraft. The only means of defense against radar-guided missiles and artillery are passive systems such as Electronic Counter Measures (ECM). Not until the end of the 1960s or beginning of the '70s were anti-radiation missiles (ARMs) developed that could be used successfully against SAM installations. Within the USAFE the 52nd Tactical Fighter Wing at Spangdahlem, Federal Republic, is totally specialized in what is known in military circles as defense suppression — the assault of enemy air defense installations. The wing is equipped with McDonnell Douglas F-4G 'Wild Weasel' combat aircraft; converted F-4E fighters brimming with advanced radar systems and electronic jamming equipment.

The term Wild Weasel was born during the Vietnam War when the USAF units fighting the air war over North Vietnam were confronted with Russian SA-2 Guideline surface-to-air missiles. American fighters were easy prey for these fast missiles and losses as a result of the North Vietnamese air defense were soon untenably high. After hundreds of fighters, mainly North American F-100 Super Sabres, were plucked out of the sky, the USAF came up with an answer. Once before, during the 'Rolling Thunder' air offensive, the USAF's fighters had been fitted with advanced ECM equipment which could disrupt enemy radar. And the two-seater F-100F Super Sabres had also been equipped with special missiles with which to assault the hostile radar installations. The F-100Fs soon handed their 'Wild Weasel' function over to the two-seater F-105G Thunderchief which had a greater flying range and could carry a heavier weapons load.

Above: The 81st Tactical Fighter Squadron of the 52nd Tactical Fighter Wing at Spangdahlem Air Base, FRG, was the first USAFE unit to receive the McDonnell Douglas F-4G Wild Weasel. This photograph was taken at Spangdahlem Air Base during the open day in June 1979. *(Cees Steijger)*

Top: During the Vietnam War Republic F-105Gs were active in the Wild Weasel role. In the seventies this type of aircraft was often deployed to European bases like Spangdahlem and Bitburg. *(Henk Koerts)*

The F-105G was, in fact, a converted F-105F recognisable by the 'cheeks' on either side of the forward fuselage section which contained the ECM equipment. Later, the F-105G was also equipped with an advanced radar-receiving system with which enemy radar frequencies could be detected. As soon as the radar installation of the North Vietnamese SAM position was activated, to intercept the intruding F-105Gs for example, the radar signal was registered by the Wild Weasel. Almost instantaneously the flight computers calculated the precise location of the SAM installation and anti-radiation missiles were launched. These missiles latched onto the radar signal transmitted by the SAM installation itself and as long as this went on working the chances of a hit were high.

Soon the F-105s were replaced by the converted McDonnell Douglas F-4C Phantoms that the 52nd TFW at Spangdahlem also used as 'Wild Weasels'. And in their turn these aircraft were replaced by the F-4G version of the Phantom. The technique remains, nevertheless, the same.

Straight through enemy lines

What is immediately striking about the F-4G is the bubble under its nose. Where the F-4E keeps its cannon the F-4G keeps its brain — the APR-38 radar. The aircraft also bristles with antennas and another visible feature is the pod under the left-hand side of the fuselage which houses the powerful ALQ-131 ECM system. Two clean General Electric J-79-GE-17 jet engines that leave hardly a trace of smoke behind them ensure that at low altitudes the aircraft is very difficult to detect with the naked eye.

All these technical facilities are needed to enable the F-4G to destroy the enemy radar stations, which are generally located well behind the frontline. The task is very demanding; on machine and pilot. As well as carrying out as strike on a heavily defended installation, the aircraft must twice run the gauntlet of the enemy lines; on its way in and, having advertised its presence by the strike, on the way out. This in the face of Soviet air defense which technologically has improved immensely since the Vietnam War. Soviet air defense radars are more accurate and faster. And many of the Warsaw pact armies' old, first-generation SA-2 Guideline air-target missiles have been replaced by advanced weapons such as the SA-5 Gammon and SA-6 Gainful.

As is only to be expected, American strategy has also been amended over the years. Thus, according to *Jane's Defence Weekly*, the tactics of the USAFE's 52nd Tactical Fighter Wing at Spangdahlem are now not so much aimed at destroying individual SAM installations but far more at putting mobile early warning radar systems out of action. By eliminating these warning systems the Warsaw Pact's air defense is blinded and the SAM installations must fall back on their own radar systems which reduces their effectiveness.

Information in pictures

Just as in all the other versions of the F-4, an F-4G's two-man crew sit tandem fashion in the cockpit; pilot in front, Electronic Warfare Officer (EWO) — responsible for navigation and operation of the APR-38 radar — behind. The plan position indicator is a vital unit in the EWO cockpit. In the centre of its radar screen the F-4 itself is displayed and around it up to fifteen different hostile 'threats' can be displayed in alphanumeric symbols.

On an attack mission, the Wild Weasel pilot flies at around 500 feet — an extremely low altitude — until within twenty to thirty kilometers of the target area and, if possible, flies around a 'racetrack' at an even lower altitude. At this low altitude the APR-38 cannot function so, periodically, the pilot must climb to give the EWO a chance to locate the enemy radars. When a radar signal is received, for example from a SA-6 Gainful, the APR-38 screen displays a '6' plus all the relevant information concerning position and distance in relation to the F-4G, at which point the pilot accelerates to around 1,100 km/h and enters the target area. When enough speed has been developed, the pilot puts the aircraft into a steep climb which brings it into position for the EWO to launch the missiles. Once the missiles are away the Wild Weasel attempts to extricate itself from the target area as fast as it can.

Although the F-4G can be equipped with virtually all the weapons normally carried by Phantoms such as Sidewinder and Sparrow air-to-air missiles and TV and radar-guided AGM-65 Mavericks, the Wild Weasels usually carry four AGM-45 Shrike or two AGM-88 HARM anti-radiation missiles. The HARM (High-speed Anti-Radiation Missile) was developed primarily for the F-4G Wild Weasel but can also be launched by the F-16.

The 52nd TFW was the third USAFE wing to switch to the F-16. That does not mean to say that the F-16s also function as Wild Weasels because at the present time only the 52nd TFW's F-4Es have been replaced. The F-16s do work together with the F-4Gs in hunter/killer operations in which the F-4G as 'hunter' locates the enemy radar with its advanced APR-38 radar and the F-16 acts as 'shooter'. Just how complicated the Wild Weasel technology is, is shown by the fact that even the F-16 can only be used in a limited way with the ARMs. The F-16C has only been able to launch the AGM-45 since 1987 and it is expected that it will take until 1991 to fully adapt the F-16's electronics for the HARM. Until then the F-4G Phantom will remain in service. According to American reports the F-4G will in any event remain in service until well into the 1990s and only then will the search for a replacement begin.

Electronic warfare

In the 1970s, the miniaturization of military electronics really took a great leap forward resulting in super-advanced micro electronics, such as the mega-chips, which have millions of connections to the square millimeter. At the same time, an almost revolutionary

Two ship formation of a F-16C and a F-4G over Germany. The two defence suppression fighters are operated by the 52nd TFW in the so-called hunter/killer role. The F-16 in the foreground is armed with AGM-45 anti-radiation missiles and two Sidewinder heat-seeking air-to-air missiles for self defence. *(General Dynamics)*

development took place in the field of computer languages, the software. This led to the technical refining of defense systems and the arrival of new intelligent weapons (smart weapons) that could find and destroy their own targets. Although the US still leads the pack in the field of electronic developments, it is generally accepted that the Soviet Union has caught up considerably, particularly in the past few years. The Russians' efforts must have produced results: advanced fighters with lookdown-shootdown radar à la Panavia Tornado and McDonnell Douglas F-15 and fire-and-forget weapons covering the entire range of laser, radar, infrared and TV guided missiles. In military circles it has been no secret for a long time that the only way to beat today's electronics — is with electronics. The term 'Electronic Warfare' was born.

Electronic Warfare puts a lot of emphasis on disruption of radar and radio installations right through to telecommunications — telephone and telex traffic. This disruption of signals, or jamming, is an Electronic Counter Measure (ECM) that is used by both the East and the West. Most ECM systems transmit a strong jamming signal that so misleads the enemy radar and surface-to-air artillery installations that they are unusable. Today's ECM systems can even produce non-existent ghost targets on the hostile radar screens. The enemy is, quite understandably, induced to fire at these ghost targets which gives aircraft equipped like the Wild Weasels a chance to detect the signal and locate and destroy a dangerous enemy system.

159

Operation 'El Dorado Canyon'

Cover for the military operation at hand was provided by 'Salty Nation' — a military exercise set up by the USAFE at great speed for that precise purpose. Within the framework of this exercise, the F-111F fighter-bombers at Lakenheath could be brought to a state of readiness without arousing comment. It also gave the USAFE an excuse for having so many extra tankers in England. In total 24 FB-111F's from Lakenheath, five EF-111A Ravens from the 42nd ECS at Upper Heyford and 28 tankers took part in the operation from England. The combined USAFE/US Navy retaliatory action was code-named 'El Dorado Canyon'.

The scenario for El Dorado Canyon was relatively simple; the F-111s would attack targets in Tripoli, the US Navy's A-6Es and A-7Es would attack targets around Benghazi and the Navy's F-14 Tomcats would cover everyone's back. The implementation was more complicated and very risky. The F-111s were faced with a round trip of more than 10,000 kilometers. On the way to the targets the heavily laden aircraft would need to refuel four times, on the way back, twice. SR-71 spy flights over the area had also shown that security along the coast and around Tripoli and Benghazi was tight. Several days before the strike there were, according to the *World Defence Almanac 1986-1987* still 252 Russian-supplied installations of which 36 were equipped with SA-5 Gammons, 72 with SA-2 Guidelines and 144 with SA-3 Goas. According to Western estimates, the Libyan Air Force also commanded around 350 mobile installations with missiles such as the SA-8 Gecko and the advanced SA-9 Gaskin. The number of radar stations was estimated at 300 of which, it was thought, around half would be operational during the strike.

During the strike the EF-111As and four EA-6B Prowlers with their powerful jammers would cripple all radar installations and communications networks (radio, telephone, telex, etc) so as to give the fighters a chance to break through the air defense. Nevertheless, so as not to take any chances, the F-111s using their terrain-following radar would fly the final phase of the run-in at around 500 feet — just outside the reach of the air defense radar.

At a quarter past six on the evening of 14 April the 28 tankers at Mildenhall and Fairford took off. They were

The Pentagon released this photo sequence of a F-111F approaching Tripoli Air Base for a bomb run.

Top: Four Il-76 transports on the platform. Note 'TTG 003' in the top right-hand corner of the photograph. (TTG means Time-to-Target.)

Middle: Il-76 photographed by F-111F strike camera: TTI 001 (Time-to-Impact).

Above: The same F-111F flies away from the target leaving three Il-76 in flames.

Top Right: F-111F viewed from a KC-135 tanker. During El Dorado Canyon the F-111s used aerial refuelling five times. *(US Air Force)*

BENINA AIRFIELD
15 APR 86

DESTROYED F-27

DAMAGED MI-8/HIP

DESTROYED MI-8/HIP

followed a short while later by five EF-111s from Upper Heyford and 24 F-111Fs from Lakenheath. Most of the F-111Fs carried a heavy bomb load of four 900 kg GBU-10 Pave Way II laser bombs or twelve conventional 500 lb bombs. Several of the F-111Fs were armed with advanced TV-guided GBU-15 Pave Strike bombs. Due to their heavy loads the first refuelling rendezvous was scheduled for over the Bay of Biscay. At that point, the six F-111Fs and one EF-111A that had flown along as tactical reserve turned back for their English bases. A short while later, five F-111s and one EF-111 were forced to return to Lakenheath because of technical problems.

The remaining 13 F-111Fs and three EF-111As carried on to their second refuelling rendezvous off the coast of Portugal then, passing over the Straits of Gibraltar at a height of 20,000 feet, flew into the Mediterranean Sea basin. The third and fourth tanker rendezvous took place off the coasts of Algeria and Tunisia. At around 23.00 hours, when the aircraft were west of Sicily, the US Navy was given the signal to move.

Libya totally surprised

According to a report of the attack in *Jane's Defence Weekly*, sometime between 23.45 and 00.15, twelve A-7Es, twelve F/A-18s, eight EA-6Bs and 24 A-6Es — two of which turned back with technical problems — were launched from the USS *America* and the USS *Coral Sea*. An unknown number of F-14 Tomcats which were to offer top cover in the target area were also launched from the USS *America*. Three US Navy E-2C AEW aircraft also remained in the air throughout the operation and patrolled east of Gibraltar and north of

Photographs of the damage inflicted by the US Navy during the attack on Benina Airfield. The photograph was taken by an SR-71 from Mildenhall, England, one day after the attack. *(DoD)*

Tripoli and Benghazi using their radars to keep an eye on the entire operation zone.

The US Navy aircraft were armed with Snakeye bombs with delay fuses and Rockeye laser bombs (A-6Es), Shrike and HARM anti-radar missiles (A-7Es and F/A-18s). The attack was opened at precisely 01.00; the A-6Es bombed the Libyan air force base at Benina and the Al Jumuhiriya barracks at Benghazi, the A-7s and F/A-18s took on the Libyan air force's coastal SAM installations.

At roughly the same time, eight F-111Fs assailed Gadaffi's Aziziya headquarters in Tripoli, the nearby Sidi Bilal training camp where, according to the US, terrorists were trained. Several minutes later the remaining F-111s attacked the military airfield at Tripoli. The Libyan forces were completely surprised by the attack. In both Tripoli and Benghazi the street lights were still burning and air defense was minimal. Only when they were being attacked on all sides did the defenders, where they were able, fire SAM missiles and the air defense artillery. At the Benina air base the MiG-23 Flogger air defense fighters could not even get off the ground because the Americans had put the runway out of action.

The actual attack ('Quick Strike') only lasted twelve minutes so the Libyans did not have much time to defend themselves. At 01.13 all the Navy pilots sent the 'Wet Legs' signal to Battle Command; they had completed the strike and were over the sea on the way back to the carriers. Twelve F-111Fs (one was shot down) and three EF-111As were also on their way home.

Above: Some of the ALQ-99E ECM-antennas of the EF-111A Raven are located in a fin-tip mounted fairing. *(Collection Cees Steijger)*

Right: One F-111F was hit by Libyan anti-aircraft artillery.The aircraft went down as a fireball. *(Cees Steijger)*

F-111 falls like a fireball

During the press conference held several days later, the Pentagon proudly announced that the surprise attacks had been a success. Only one F-111F had been shot down by air-target artillery — and not five as the Russian press agency TASS had tried to convince the world. The aircraft, with Captain Pilot Fernando L. Ribas-Dominicci and Weapons Systems Officer Paul F. Lorence on board, was hit shortly after the attack on Gadaffi's headquarters and, according to Western eye-witnesses in Tripoli, went down 'like a fireball' into the sea.

One other, harmless, incident occurred on the return journey to England when the engines of one of the F-111s started overheating shortly after refuelling off the coast of Algeria and the crew decided to divert to Rota air base, Spain. The rest of the air fleet flew back without any problems and after one more refuelling rendezvous west of Portugal the F-111Fs landed at their English bases at around 06.00. Two hours later the last KC-10A landed at Mildenhall after fourteen hours in the air.

During the morning of 15 April, an SR-71 of the 9th Strategic Reconnaissance Wing from Beale AFB, California, which was on a Detachment 4 posting in England, took off on a reconnaissance flight over the target areas. One of the photographs published by the Pentagon showed the result of the Navy's attack on the air base at Benina very clearly; bomb craters on the runways, four totally destroyed MiG-23 Floggers and what were probably more MiG-23s in a completely ruined hangar. At the military airfield in Tripoli five completely destroyed Ilyushin IL-76 transports and several badly damaged aircraft including a Fokker F-27 were counted. The Al Jumuhiriya barracks in Benghazi were severely damaged as were the Aziziya barracks in Tripoli. Only the Sidi Bilal training camp survived almost intact.

★   ★   ★

A lethal video game

From a military point of view the American retaliatory attack on Libya was a success although some Western commentators asked why the USAFE's F-111Fs from England had been involved in the strike on Tripoli. It was even suggested that the motive behind using these aircraft was not military necessity but political expediency. Whether this was the reason is, naturally, difficult to prove. One can better ask why F-111s were used for a risky strike on distant Libyan targets. Especially as it may be assumed that the US Navy — which had two aircraft carriers lurking in Libya's front garden — could easily have carried out the attack on Tripoli. Or was the Tripoli strike a sort of practical test of the air force's advanced strike instruments? Whatever it was, with this daring action the USAFE again proved its night-time precision bombing capability made possible by advanced laser and infrared technology.

During the last decade the Americans have made great strides in these technologies and for the last few years laser/infrared apparatus has been installed in most F-111 fighter-bombers of the 3rd Air Force in England. The heart of the laser/infrared installation is the AN/AVQ-26 Pave Tack target-location system developed by Ford Aerospace & Communications. Its

extremely sensitive laser and infrared cameras can find the target even in thick fog or during a snow storm. In the F-111 the Pave Tack equipment is fitted in a streamlined nacelle housed in the bomb bay. Along with Pave Tack the aircraft can carry a maximum of four 900 kg laser- or TV-guided bombs; generally GBU-10 Pave Way II laser bombs or GBU-15 Pave Strike TV-guided bombs. The system is operated by the 'whizzo' — the Weapons Systems Officer in popular American air force parlance.

Before each mission the Weapons Systems Officer studies reconnaissance photographs to familiarize himself with the distinguishing features of the targets and their surrounding areas and then programmes the details into Texas Instruments AN/APQ-119 navigation computer. As the F-111 approaches the target area the whizzo lowers the nacelle containing the Pave Tack equipment out of the bomb bay. The radars and TV cameras immediately start scanning the horizon to locate the pre-programmed target. When the aircraft is within ninety seconds of the target the pilot dives to 500 feet and accelerates to over 1,000 km/h. The Pave Tack system continues producing razor sharp video images of the target area which are displayed on the monitor in the whizzo's cockpit. He locates the target and 'fires' a laser beam at it (target painting). The computer locks-on and continuously recalculates the remaining distance to the target. At less than a minute away from the target the pilot presses the button on the side-stick which activates the bomb-release computer. The computer then calculates the correct moment at which the laser bombs must be released. Once the bombs are away the pilot pulls the F-111 into a vertical climb in order to get out of the target area as quickly as possible. Meanwhile, the Pave Tack's laser remains fixed on the target and the bombs follow the beam to the bitter end. A 'hit' is almost certain because the Pave Way II laser bombs have a directional accuracy to within just a few meters which means even relatively small targets, such as bunkers, can be attacked with deadly accuracy.

The F-111s are not the only USAFE aircraft in which Pave Tack can be installed. The 52nd TFW's McDonnell Douglas F-4G Wild Weasels at Spangdahlem, FRG, can also be equipped with the system. And in the near future LANTIRN (Low Altitude Navigation/Targetting Infrared for Night) laser equipment will be installed in the USAFE's F-16s. LANTIRN is standard equipment in the McDonnell Douglas F-15E Eagle — the USAF's latest fighter-bomber.

★　　★　　★

Above: The first McDonnell Douglas KC-10 Extenders for the Libyan attack arrived as soon as 11 April 1986 at Mildenhall and Fairford. *(Collection Cees Steijger)*

Top: Lockheed EC-130H Compass Call are flying jammers and stationed at Sembach Air Base, FRG. Little is known of the exact missions of these electronic transports. *(Collection Cees Steijger)*

Yankee go home!

Shortly after the attack on Libya, Spanish Premier Felipe Gonzalez stated categorically that none of the four American bases in Spain had been used for the operation. But an F-111 on the way back to England from Tripoli did divert to the American marine support post at Rota near Cadiz with engine trouble. The aircraft landed a few hours after the attack and remained for two days while the engines were thoroughly checked.

Gonzalez may have diplomatically looked the other way, the Spanish people did not. As soon as news of the attack appeared in the media there were mass protests against the military adventure in the streets of Madrid and Barcelona. Anti-American factions in the capital exploited the situation and several thousand demonstrators were soon assembled around the American embassy chanting 'Yankee go home'. This was by no means an isolated incident. Since General Franco's death and the restoration of democracy in 1975, hardly an opportunity for a demonstration against the American presence in Spain had been missed.

Extensive American presence in Spain dated from 1953 when Franco gave the US permission not only to use several Spanish bases but also to build the large Torrejon air base, 22 kilometers from Madrid. Torrejon was at the centre of the anti-American and anti-NATO demonstrations, especially after USAFE's 401st Tactical Fighter Wing at Torrejon took delivery of 79 General Dynamics F-16s. The Director of the Spanish Ministry of Information, Inocencio Arias, made no secret of the fact that for the Spanish people the base was a symbol of Franco's mistakes. In an interview with the American newspaper, the *Wall Street Journal*, he explained that as far as the Spaniards were concerned the Spanish dictator should never have permitted the US to build such an extensive base — its 4.5-kilometer runway is the longest in Europe — so close to Madrid when it could just as well have been sited in a thinly populated region of the Spanish hinterland. According to public opinion, the fact that it was built where it was proved that its prime purpose was to support Franco, who at the time had his headquarters in Madrid.

Spain's joining of NATO in May 1981 was also strongly criticized and in 1986 there was even a referendum concerning the country's continued membership of NATO. The referendum was held at the request of Premier Gonzalez in fulfillment of an election promise made by the socialist party during the election campaign of 1981. Against all expectations a small majority (53 per cent) voted for continued membership but only on three conditions which effectively limited Spain's participation in the alliance. First and foremost, Spain would not participate in the military command of NATO. Secondly, the law forbidding the installation and storage of nuclear weapons in Spain would remain in force. And thirdly, and this was the key-condition in the eyes of defense specialists, the American military presence in Spain was to be reduced.

The F-16s MUST go

At the beginning of 1987 there was an estimated 12,000 American military personnel in Spain. Around 5,000 were based at Rota, the large marine base near Cadiz which is an essential support post for the American 6th Fleet. The remaining personnel were based at Torrejon, Zaragoza and Moron air bases and at several smaller bases — primarily radar stations and observation posts — spread throughout the country. Had Madrid so desired, it could have ended all military presence simply by not renewing the 1953 bilateral agreement which was for a period of 35 years. But the situation was not that simple.

In the US's eyes, Spain is a full member of NATO and therefore has joint responsibility for security in this strategically very important region of the alliance. Moreover, the Spanish air force — the Ejercito del Aire — is part of NATO's 6th Allied Tactical Air Force (ATAF) in southern Europe and in time of war must also accept responsibility for the air defense of Italy, Greece and Turkey. The US took the view that if Gonzalez could not fully discharge these responsibilities he could do no other than accept America's use of the Spanish bases.

On 16 March 1987 during a summit meeting in Madrid, Caspar Weinberger, the former American

Secretary of Defense, tried without success to talk the Spanish Premier round. Felipe Gonzalez made the US's willingness to relinquish Torrejon air base conditional to the renewal of the bilateral agreement. If the US did not comply, argued the Spanish Defense Minister Narcis Serra later, then the renewal of the agreement would not go ahead and as far as he was concerned all the American military units could go home. The result of this policy is now clear; the Americans had to climb down and agreed to the evacuation of Torrejon. This did at least secure them continued use of the Rota Marine Base and the Zaragoza and Moron air bases. And even Torrejon is not totally barred to the Americans because as a stand-by base it will still be available for deployments and for use in times of crisis.

Spanish air force takes on NATO duties

The agreement is that the 401st TFW's F-16s must be out of Torrejon by 1992. This means that the Spanish air force must prepare to take over the American F-16s' NATO duties. The main tasks are the support of the Italian, Greek and Turkish armed forces and this will involve regular exercises in these countries. The Spanish air force will, therefore, have to take an active role in NATO exercises in southern Europe such as 'Display Determination' and 'Dawn Patrol'. The big question is whether the Spanish defense budget can bear the additional $75 million burden it is estimated that taking on these NATO duties will cost.

To fulfill its NATO responsibilities, the Spanish air force intends replacing its old F-4C Phantom fighters stationed at Torrejon, which date from 1964, with 36 of the 72 advanced McDonnell Douglas F/A-18 Hornet

The F-16s from the 401st TFW at Torrejon had to leave.
(General Dynamics)

fighters Spain ordered some time ago. This will mean a fifty per cent reduction in fighting power because however advanced the Hornet may be, 36 of them will, obviously, never be able to do the work of 79 F-16s. In defense circles it is also being whispered that the new Hornets will be used exclusively for Spain's own defense and will make no contribution to NATO's air defense.

The US could do little else than attempt to find their F-16s an alternative base somewhere in the Mediterranean region. Both Portugal and Turkey were considered initially — although the *Wall Street Journal* reported that Belgium was also under consideration. The Moroccan Sidi Slimane and Kenitra airfields were also mentioned as possibles. Washington let it be known that if no alternative European base was found for the F-16s the only alternative would be to recall them to the US and disband the combat unit. This would reduce the strength of the USAFE by around ten per cent; a bloodletting which would seriously weaken NATO's southern flank. The Spanish decision to deport the American F-16s was, therefore, no longer a purely American concern but rather a NATO matter. The American Department of Defense dropped the entire problem into the laps of the NATO ministers in Brussels.

In the summer of 1988, after much haggling and indecision, the southern Italian Crotone air base was designated as the new F-16 base. The base had lain empty for nine years and NATO had to foot the bill for rebuilding and refurbishing. Their NATO ally Spain's decision cost the European taxpayers $500 million.

A close formation of four McDonnell Douglas F-15C interceptors of the 32nd TFS at Soesterberg, the Netherlands. *(McDonnell Douglas)*

Greece turns against the US

Although both Greece and Turkey are members of NATO, the two countries squabble openly and often about their rights in the Aegean Sea and the status of Cyprus. For the past twenty years the two countries have hovered on the brink of war. Tension escalated in July 1974 when a Turkish invasion force landed on Cyprus and, after heavy fighting against the Greek-Cypriot National Guard, occupied the north-eastern part of the island. NATO stepped in and defused the situation but this did not solve the Greek-Turkish question.

Relations between the two countries remained strained and in March 1987 suddenly degenerated into a new crisis. The direct cause was Turkey's attempt to use the seismological exploration vessel *Sismik-1* to search for oil in the Aegean. Greece, which considers the Aegean part of their own territory, threatened military intervention if Ankara violated Greek rights. At the same time the Greek Premier, Andreas Papandreou, banned the Americans from the listening post at Nea Makri, in the north of Greece. Luckily Ankara, under pressure from NATO, ceased explorations in the contested area, whereupon the crisis died down as quickly as it had arisen. The Greek government's adamant attitude during this crisis was remarkable, as was their decision to evacuate the American Makri base. Granted the decision was reversed as soon as the crisis was over, but it is still surprising that in Greece the American military presence goes on the agenda every time the country is at odds with its eastern neighbour.

Papandreou's juggling trick

Greece's parliamentary elections of autumn 1981 revolved almost entirely around foreign policy. Socialist leader Andreas Papandreou's victory was, to a great extent, subscribed to his electoral promise to close the four American bases and put the country's NATO membership on the agenda for re-consideration.

In 1953, shortly after Greece joined NATO, the US was permitted to use Greek bases to support USAFE reconnaissance flights in the Middle East and North Africa and to facilitate observation of Soviet activities in the eastern Mediterranean. For many years the SAC operated RC-135 reconnaissance aircraft and EC-135 airborne command posts from the Hellenikon air base near Athens and the Iraklion air base on Crete while the American 6th Fleet made intensive use of the Souda Bay Marine Base, also on Crete. Little came of Papandreou's promise because exactly two years after his election he signed a new Defense and Economic Co-operation Agreement (DECA) with Washington and shortly afterwards extended the period of use of the four bases by five years. In Athens Papandreou's 'modus operandi' was hailed as a good juggling trick by which to take power. His supporters obviously did not object because he was re-elected in June 1985.

According to political observers the question of Greece's NATO membership and the US's use of the Greek bases is extremely complicated. Although Greece is the most anti-NATO of all the NATO member states, its resignation from NATO is almost impossible. Indeed, Greece's resignation from NATO would put an end to any further American aid. It might also mean that Turkey would become NATO's 'enfant cherie' and that is precisely what Greece wants to prevent at all costs.

American use of Hellenikon air base near Athens remained disputable. But times are changing. As part of the American plan to shut down one hundred installations worldwide — in response to the changes in Eastern Europe — the Bush administration in January 1990 proposed the closure of both Hellenikon and the navy communications facility Nea Makri on the east coast of Attica.

★　★　★

USAFE exposed to terror

The USAFE has not only had to face political resistance but in some countries has faced far more violent resistance from various terrorist groups whose method of expressing their displeasure is to bomb American military installations. Such was the case on 8 August 1985 when a car bomb was set off at the Rhein Main air base, killing two American servicemen and severely wounding twenty others. Responsibility for this attack was claimed by the German Rote Armee Faction (RAF) which works in co-operation with the French Action Directe. In a letter to several press agencies the perpetrators stated that the attack had been carried out by the 'Kommando Jackson'. (George Jackson, the idol of both terrorist organizations, was a militant black American who was shot dead by guards while attempting to escape from St. Quentin high security prison. Jackson was a member of the Soledad Brothers and had several terrorist attacks to his 'credit'.) The reason given for the reprehensible attack on Rhein Main was that it was 'pivotal for the war in

A car bomb exploded at Rhein Main Air Base on 8 August 1985 killing two people and injuring eleven others. The bomb went off between the 435th Tactical Airlift Wing headquarters and a base-dormitory at the time when people were arriving for work at the base. (ANP)

the Third World and a nest for the intelligence services'. The bomb used in the bloody attack was a home-made device containing hundreds of railway sleeper nuts which resulted in a 'splinter effect'. The same type of car bomb was also used in the summer of 1981 at Ramstein — the USAFE's headquarters.

★　★　★

Epilogue

The effects of the developments in Spain and Greece can very easily spill over into other countries where the US has bases. In February 1987, an article appeared in the *Wall Street Journal* under the headline 'First Domino?'. In it an anonymous NATO spokesman warned that the Spanish and Greek developments could cause a domino effect. Italy, they indicated tentatively, may be the next NATO member state to close down American military installations within its borders. Particularly now that support for the Italian communists is growing, the future of American presence seems less certain; however, the decision to open Crotone to the 401st TFW's F-16s may suggest the opposite.

In Great Britain too, a change of political course may also result in the USAFE being asked to withdraw. The Labour party is apparently committed to closing the American bases in the UK if elected.

committees which have been frustrated by the lack of progress in their inquiries.

Congress would hold off granting immunity to the other key witness in the scandal, Marine Lt Col Oliver North, and would delay summoning

criticised the President's management and policy of selling arms to Iran in return for US hostages held in Lebanon, but both the House and Senate select committees are under pressure to uncover more details in order to justify their existence.

viewing another figure in the affair, Mr Adnan Khashoggi, the Saudi billionaire.

Mr Marlin Fitzwater, White House spokesman, said that documents had been received which fitted descriptions of notes made by Ms Walters.

Weinberger told F-16 fighters must be withdrawn from Spain

BY TOM BURNS IN MADRID

MR CASPAR Weinberger, the US Defence Secretary, was told in Madrid yesterday that the Socialist Government of Mr Felipe Gonzalez is insisting on the withdrawal of F-16 jet-fighters from Spain as a precondition for the renewal of the US-Spanish defence pact which expires in May next year.

Mr Weinberger arrived in Madrid on Sunday night with Assistant Secretary Richard Perle, who resigned his post last week. It is the first leg of a tour of Nato's southern flank, which also includes a visit to Turkey and a stopover, on the way back to Washington, at the US air base on Portugal's Azores Islands.

Both Turkey and Portugal have been suggested as possible alternative sites for the 79 F-16 interceptors of the US 401st tactical air wing which are currently stationed at Torrejon base, eight miles north east of Madrid.

Mr Perle told Spanish journalist at the Pentagon last week that the Torrejon fighters were "irreplacible and vital" to Nato, and that their withdrawal from Spain would "weaken security in the entire mediterranean." The F-16'S operational

zone stretches to Turkey.

In talks yesterday with Mr Gonzalez and Mr Narcis Serra, the Spanish Defence Minister, Mr Weinberger and his party were told that the Government was committed to bring about a "substantial reduction," in US personnel and installations in Spain under the terms of a referendum a year ago in which Spaniards voted to remain in Nato.

This broad aim has been narrowed down to a specific demand for the withdrawal of the Torrejon fighters. Failure to agree on this would jeopardise the renewal of the bilateral agreement and could force a total US withdrawal from Spain.

At present, the US has facilities at two airbases, in addition to Torrejon, and it maintains a naval depot at Rota, near Cadiz. The bilateral agreement, which dates from 1953 and is renewed every five years, allows for a maximum 12,500 US servicemen in Spain.

An offer by the US last month to remove the 401st tactical air wing from the Madrid area to a base at Moron, near Seville, was rejected outright by the Spanish team nego-

tiating renewal of the bilateral agreement.

The US Ambassador to Madrid said at the time that the offer represented "a maximum effort" to accommodate Madrid's demands. The Spanish negotiators stressed that the interceptors had to leave Spain altogether.

Mr Weinberger said on arrival at Madrid that he hoped to depart with "better terms" for the bilateral agreement. Coincidentally, his aircraft touched down just hours after violence erupted at the end of the seventh annual protest march to the Torrejon airbase which draws tens of thousands every year.

The Turkish Government last night released details of the defence and economic agreements signed yesterday with the US, on the eve of Mr Weinberger's visit to Ankara.

The signing of the agreements comes just under 15 months after the previous US-Turkish defence agreement expired.

The text as published does not suggest that the US has made any major concessions, even though

Continued on Page 28

Continued on Page 28

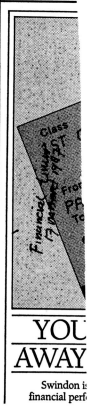

YOU
AWAY

Swindon i: financial perf

Clipping from *Financial Times*, 17 March 1987.

Such developments contain a great hidden danger; NATO's air power would be so weakened that some of the fingers on the Soviet buttons may get itchy. Withdrawal of the American troops from Europe would leave gaps that the NATO member states could not possibly fill. The USAFE alone, with its 800 aircraft and 70,000 personnel, is larger than the combined air forces of Belgium, Denmark and the Netherlands.

But there are exceptions: in the Netherlands, for example, the USAFE appears to have an unshakeable position. The situation in the Netherlands is somewhat unique. Since 1954, the 32nd TFS stationed at Soesterberg air base (Camp New Amsterdam), has been under the command of the Dutch air force. The squadron's F-15C Eagles are a permanent element in the Dutch air defense. During interception missions they, like the F-16s of the Koninklijke Luchtmacht (KLu), receive their orders from Dutch commanders at the Combat Reporting Centre in Nieuw-Milligen — or 'Dutch-Mill' as the Americans call it.

Colonel Albert E. Pruden, Squadron Commander of the 32nd TFS at the time the switch was made from F-4 Phantoms to F-15 Eagles, once said that the close co-operation between the KLu and the USAFE should form an example for all the other NATO member states. Both parties benefit from the unique situation. For contributing infrastructure and support units, the KLu's air defense is considerably strengthened. Quite rightly, Pruden doubted whether the Dutch air force could ever afford such expensive interceptors as the F-15s. Purchasing the F-15s to equip a single squadron would cost billions of Dutch guilders and the yearly operating costs run into millions. Too much for such a small air force.

The Pentagon's policy clearly points towards the European integration of the USAFE. Economically at least. And very probably prompted by the politicians in Bonn. At the beginning of the 1980s, for example, the USAFE placed an extensive order for hundreds of mini-buses and Passat private cars with Volkswagen AG in Wolfsburg. Whether the American military were overjoyed at having to exchange their comfortable Chevvies and Dodges for Teutonic austerity is doubtful. It is equally doubtful whether the pilots of the 10th Military Airlift Squadron at Zweibrücken were happy with their Short Brothers C-23A Sherpa transports. The acquisition of eighteen of these small aircraft — less than affectionally known as 'flying shoe boxes' — clearly bore the stamp of pressure from on high.

Although the USAFE organization has undergone several upheavals during the past forty years and has had to bend with the wind of political pressure both from the US and Europe, its prime objective remains unchanged; to ensure the continuing security and freedom of Western Europe. Furthering this objective has not always been easy; mistakes have been made and the result has not always been a thing of beauty. But, as the old saying goes, 'beauty is only skin deep'. It is the intention behind the objective that is, and always has been most important: the intention to be ready whenever and for whatever is necessary. The USAFE's actions have been humanitarian, such as in Berlin during the blockade. They have been provocative, such as during the building of the Berlin Wall. They have also been vengeful, such as in Libya in 1986. The prime responsibility for the preservation of the security and freedom of Western Europe rests with NATO. Within NATO's theatre of operations there is an important role for the USAFE.

Appendix
Major USAFE Organizations

While the USAFE command underwent many mission changes over the years following the conclusion of World War II, its primary reason for existence remained defense of the peace and freedom of Western Europe. The successful achievement of this mission is a lasting testimony to the many Air Force men and women who have dedicated years of service to the continued preservation of democracy at home and abroad.

Third Air Force

USAFE's command for the United Kingdom since May 1951. Originally established at South Ruislip Air Station near London, Third Air Force superseded 3rd Air Division as the United States Air Force began its great build up in the United Kingdom. The headquarters moved to RAF Mildenhall in June 1972, where it functions as the single point of contact with the British government for USA forces in the United Kingdom as well as providing area and logistical support. The following units are assigned to Third Air Force:

10th Tactical Fighter Wing, RAF Alconbury, UK. Stationed here since August 1959, the 10th TFW originally joined USAFE in July 1952 when it was activated as 10th Tactical Reconnaissance Wing at Toul-Rosières Airbase, France. In May 1953 it moved to Spangdahlem Airbase, Germany, where its mission expanded to include electronic warfare as well as reconnaissance.

Although reduced to one reconnaissance squadron of RF-4Cs in 1976, at the same time it acquired a second mission of operating F-5E aggressors of the 527th Aggressor Squadron. Nowadays the 10th TFW has two squadrons of A-10 Thunderbolts and acts as host for the Lockheed TR-1 reconnaissance aircraft of the SAC's 95th Reconnaissance Squadron.

20th Tactical Fighter Wing, RAF Upper Heyford, UK. Activated at Shaw Air Force Base, South Carolina, in August 1947, the 20th Fighter Bomber Wing was deployed with F-84s to RAF Wethersfield, England, in May 1952. It was the first USAFE fighter unit capable of using tactical nuclear weapons. Re-equipped with F-100s in 1957, it was renamed a tactical fighter wing in 1958. It moved to its present location in April 1970 and converted its three fighter squadrons to F-111Es.

The 20th Tactical Fighter Wing supports the EF-111A Raven Electronic Warfare aircraft of the 42nd Electronic Combat Squadron that is assigned to the 66th Electronic Combat Wing at Sembach Airbase, Germany.

48th Tactical Fighter Wing, RAF Lakenheath, UK. Activated in July 1952 as the 48th Fighter Bomber Wing at Chaumont Airbase, France, it was originally equipped with F-84Gs. Later in the decade it used various bases in Germany as forward operating locations. In 1960 the 48th moved to RAF Lakenheath where it began the transition from the F-100 to the F-4 in 1972. Five years later it converted to four squadrons of F-111Fs.

81st Tactical Fighter Wing, RAF Bentwaters/Woodbridge, UK. The 81st Fighter Wing came to USAFE in September 1951 with the command's first F-86s. Although its squadrons were originally assigned to three separate bases, the wing headquarters has remained at RAF Bentwaters since 1951. In July 1958 the renamed 81st Tactical Fighter Wing also assumed control of RAF Woodbridge, thereafter operating it and Bentwaters as a 'Twin base'. After flying F-84Fs, F-101s, and F-4s, the 81st began converting to A-10s in 1978. The wing keeps aircraft at a forward operating location in Germany.

513th Airborne Command and Control Wing, RAF Mildenhall, UK. Six weeks after being activated at Evreux-Fauville Airbase, France, in April 1966, the 513th Troop Carrier Wing moved to RAF Mildenhall with two rotational C-130 squadrons. Renamed a tactical airlift wing in 1967, the 513th's mission included operation of USEUCOM airborne command post aircraft. In 1976 MAC absorbed the wing's C-130 mission, leaving the 513th with the 10th Airborne Command and Control Squadron, which operates EC-135 Airborne Command Posts, and growing host unit responsibilities at RAF Mildenhall.

527th Aggressor Squadron, RAF Bentwaters, UK. USAFE activated the 527th Aggressor Squadron at RAF Alconbury on 1 April 1976. Originally designated 527th Tactical Fighter training aggressor squadron the unit was assigned to the 10th TRW to conduct Dissimilar Air Combat Training (DACT) for fighter and reconnaissance aircrews. The squadron operated

C–133 Cargomaster   104
EB–66E Destroyer   116, *116*, 118
RB–66C   105–6, 107, *107*
Dreux-Semonches air base   77, 99, *100*, 100
dual-basing principle   112
Duxford air base   *39, 56*

E

Eaker, Brigadier General Ira C.   35, 36, *36*, 38, 41, 47
Edwards Air Force Base   150
Eglin Air Force Base   *10*, 12
Egypt   89, 91, 121–2
Eielson Air Force Base   19
Eighth (8th) Air Force   35, 36, 38, 48–52
Eisenhower, General Dwight D.   49, 53, 60
El Dorado Canyon, Operation   126, 164–5
electronic warfare   106, 116, 118, 159–60
Elmendorf Air Force Base   *17*, 18
Enola Gay (B–29)   *11*
Escadrille Americaine   25–6
Escadrille Lafayette   26–7
Etain-Rouvres air base   77, 92, 99
Europe
    proposed integration of USAFE   172
    resistance to US military presence   108
European Army proposal   86–7
European Defense Alliance (EDA)   87
European Tanker Task Force (ETTF)   147, 148
Evreux-Fauville air base   77
Extraversion test programme   58

F

Fairchild
    A–10 Thunderbolt II   19, 22, 136–7, *138*, 160
    C–82   67
Fairford air base   84, 114, 147, 148, 163, *168*
Fifteenth (15th) Air Force   47, 48, 50, 52
Fifth (5th) Air Force   19
Flag exercise programmes   13, 134
Flexible Response strategy   94, 104, 113
Florennes air base   154
flying jammers   116, 118, 143, 160, *168*
France
    attitude towards NATO   110
    and German rearmament   86, 87
    independent nuclear capability   110
    Suez Canal crisis   91
    US air bases   77
    US nuclear bases   92
    withdrawal of US air bases   110–11
Frankfurt   31
Freloc, Operation   110–11
Fuerstenfeldbruck air base   57, 64, 68, *88*

G

Gabriel, General Charles A.   163
Gadaffi, Muammar   119, 161–2
Gatow air base   66
Gaulle, Charles de   87, 92, 110
General Dynamics
    BGM–109G Tomahawk   154, *156*
    F–16 Fighting Falcon   13, *14*, 19, 22, 135, 148–9, *150*, 150–1, *152, 153*, 159, 169, *169*
    F–16A   *10, 17*, 139, 143, *148*
    F–16C   *144, 159*
    F–111   114, 115–16, *116*, 135–6, 139, *139*, 147, 149, 163, 164, *164*, 165, 166, *166*, 167
Geneva summit   88, 89
Germany (*see also* Berlin; West Germany)
    aircraft production (WW II)   45
    cities bombed   34
    rearmament question   86
    strikes against aircraft industries   48
    U-boat attacks   31
    World War I   25–8
    Yalta conference   53
Giebelstadt air base   57, 68
GIN-gap   141
Gonzalez, Felipe   168–9
Goose Bay air base   *85*, 98
Grafton Underwood air base   36
Grand Slam exercise   101–2
Greece   59–60, 170–1
Greek Action, Operation   122
Greenham Common air base   84, 92, 147, 154
Groom Dry Lake Air Force Base   23, 128

group bombing   37–8
Grumman
    EA–6B Prowler   160, 164
    F–14 Tomcat   116, 161, *161*, 164, 165
Grumman/General Dynamics EF–111A Raven   118, *160*, 160–1, 164–5, *166*
Gulf of Sirte   161

H

H-bomb   83, 109–10
Hahn air base   92, 110, 111, 112, 129, *148*–9, 152, *153*
Harris, Air Chief Marshal Arthur   34, 36
headquarters   122
Heinkel, He 162   53
Hellenikon air base   161, 170
Hickman Air Force Base   19
Hill Air Force Base   *10, 17*, 136, 137
Holloman Air Force Base   136
Hughes APG-63 radar   131
Hungary, Soviet invasion of   *91*, 92

I

Iceland   12–13, 141, 142
Ilyushin
    Il–18   142
    Il–27   89
    Il–76   *164*
Incirlik air base   82, 112, 125
industrial bombing targets (WW II)   36, 39, 40, 41, 42–3, 44, *46*, 48–9, 50–1, 52
Iran   143–4, 146, 147
Israel   91, 119–22
Italy   87, 163, 169, 171

J

Japan   16, 31
Johnson, Lyndon B.   110, 114, 126–7

K

Keesler Air Force Base   146
Keflavik air base   13, 141, 142
Kennedy, John F.   94, 95, 96, 97, 102, 103
Khrushchev, Nikita   95
Kitzingen air base   57
Korat air base   20
Kunsan air base   *14*, 19, 151

L

Lajes air base   98, 103
Lakenheath air base   68, 92, 136, 151, 164, 165
Landstuhl air base (*see also* Ramstein air base)   77, 88
Langley, Samuel Pierpont   9
Langley Air Force Base   11, *13*, 129
LANTIRN (Low Altitude Navigation/Targeting Infrared for Night) system   18, 167
Laon-Couvon air base   77, 92, 110
Lechfeld air base   52, 53
Leeuwarden air base   *148*
LeMay, General Curtis   36, 37, 41, 44, 83
Lend-Lease Act   30, 54
Libya
    aggressive foreign policy   161–2
    strike against   126, *162, 163*, 163–6, *164, 165, 166*
    terrorist activities   162, *162*
    withdrawal of US bases   119
Limited Nuclear Response   94
Line of Death (Gulf of Sirte)   161
Linebacker, Operation   20
Lockheed
    A–12   126–7
    AC–130U Spectre   18
    C–5 Galaxy   18, 20, 100, 120, 144
    C–130 Hercules   18, 20, 120, 144, 146, 147, *148*
    C–130A–II   82, *82*, 122
    C–141 Starlifter   *11*, 18. 20, 104, 120, *154*, 154
    C–5 Galaxy   18, 20, 100, 120, 144
    EC–130H Compass Call   118, 160, *168*
    F–104 Starfighter   96, 97–8
    F–104A Starfighter   99–100
    F–104C   *99, 101*, 103, *104*
    F–117A   23, *24*
    MC–130E Combat Talon   18, 122, *122*, 124, *126*
    MC–130H Combat Talon II   18
    P–38 Lightning   *44, 46*, 50
    P–80 Shooting Star   59, 64
    SR–71 Blackbird   121, *122*

SR–71A Blackbird   125, 126, *127*, 127–8
T–33 Shooting Star   73, *77*, 88, *88*, 98
TR–1   126, 143
TR–1A   155, *155*, 156, 160
U–2   124, 125, *125*, 126, *128*, 155
YP–80A Shooting Star   58, *61*
LTV, A–7D   *24*
Luftwaffe
   destruction of   52
   disarmament   53

M

Marham air base   68, 147
McDill Air Force Base   7, *74*, 110, 151
McDonnell
   F4H Phantom (*see also under* McDonnell Douglas)   107–8, *108*
   RF–101 Voodoo   20, 107
McDonnell Douglas
   F–4 Phantom   13, 112, *113*, 115, 128, *138, 139*, 151, *151*
   F–4E   22, *118, 119*, 120, *121*, 129, *131*, 142, *149*
   F–4G   *23*
   F–4G Wild Weasel   22, 156, *158*, 158–9, *159*, 167
   F–15 Eagle   *17*, 19, 22, 103, *136, 140*
   F–15A   128–9, *130, 131*, 143
   F–15C   *11*, 13, *14, 129*, 130, 131, *134, 137, 142*, 143, *170*, 172
   F–15E   167
   F/A–18 Hornet   169
   KC–10 Extender   21, 163, *168*
   RF–4C   *24*, 107, *111*, 139, 155
McNamara, Robert   115
Market Garden, Operation   51
Martin
   B–26 Marauder   39, 40, 41, *45*
   B–57 Canberra   16, 20, 107
   EB–57E   116, 118, *120*
Massive Response defense strategy   93, 94, 96
Mediterranean Allied Air Forces (MAAF)   47
Messerschmitt
   Me 163 Komet   52
   Me 262   52, 53
Mikoyan
   MiG–15   77, 78, 79, 89, 128
   MiG–21   22, 128, 134
   MiG–23   22, 134, *140*
   MiG–25   128, 130
   MiG–29   22, 135, 148
   MiG–31   22
Mildenhall air base   110, 111, 114, *124*, 125, 129, 144, 146, 147, *148*, 163, 166, *168*
Military Air Command (MAC)   104, 176
Military Air Transport Service (MATS)   67, 104
Military Airlift Command (MAC)   18, 119, 120
Military Defense Identification Zone (MADIZ)   141, 142
Misawa air base   19
Mitchell, Brigadier General William   28, 29, *30*
modernization programmes   22, 76, 94, 107–8, 115, 128, 135, 143
Molesworth air base   154
Moron air base   98, *99*, 103, *104, 106*, 111
Mountain Home Air Force Base   136
Multinational Operational Test and Evaluation team (MOT&E)   150
Mutual Defense Assistance Program (MDAP)   73, 88
Myasishchyev, M–4   83

N

Nasser, Colonel   89
NATO (North Atlantic Treaty Organization)
   combined forces   21, 136
   cruise missiles   153, 143
   establishment   73
Nellis Air Force Base   134, 136
Netherlands   172
Neuburg air base   52
Neubiburg air base   64
Neutrality Act   30, 31
Nieuport fighter aircraft   26, *26*
Ninth (9th) Air Force   47
Nixon, Richard   121
Noervenich air base   152
North American
   AT–6, 60, *60*, 73
   B–45 Tornado   76, 82, 84, *85, 86*
   F–86 Sabre   73, 80, *80*, 88, 101, 128
   F–86H Sabre   96, 97, 102, *102*
   F–100 Super Sabre   13, 20, 92, *92*, 96, 103
   F–100F Super Sabre   156
   P–51 Mustang   50, 52, *56*
   P–51B Mustang   46–7, *48*

P–51D   *49*
T–39 Sabreliner   105
North American Air Defense Command (NORAD)   18–19, *19*, 142
Northern Wedding exercises   139, 142
Northrop
   B–2   16, 23
   F–5E Tiger II   *10*, 13, 134, 135, *136, 140*
   F–89 Scorpion   142
Norway   139–40
nuclear accidents   109–10
nuclear deterrence   16, 93–4
nuclear diplomacy   93
nuclear weapons depots   152–3

O

objectives of USAFE   172
Oksboel exercise   118
Operational Detachment Delta   144
Overlord, Operation   49

P

Pacific Air Force (PACAF)   19–20
Palomares incident   *109*, 109–10
Panama   23
Panavia Tornado   22
Pathfinder Force (PFF)   49
Pave Tack system   136, 166–7
Pearl Harbor   31
Pershing 2 missiles   143, 154
Peterson Air Force Base   18
Phalsbourg-Bourscheid air base   77, 99, 101
pilots' training (*see also* combat exercises)   119, 134–5
Pléven Plan   86
Pointblank, Operation   41
Poland   53–4
Polebrooke air base   *36*, 36
Potsdam conference   54, 60
powered flight, early   9
precision bombing   34–5, 38, 136, 166–7
Precision Locator Strike System (PLSS)   155, 156

Q

Quick Reaction Alert (QRA) bases   153
Quick Reaction Force   100–1

R

radar systems   18–19, 107, 125, 131, 156
Rammjager   52
Ramstein air base   76, 77, 95, 100, 111, *118*, 122, 125, 129, 144, *148, 150*, 152, 153
Rapid Reinforcement capability   104, 138
Ready Eagle project   129
Ready Switch project   136
Reagan, Ronald   162
reconnaissance and surveillance   56, 78, 82, 88, 103, 105–6, 121, 124, 125–8, 155–6
recovery system   18, 122, 124
Red Flag exercises   13, 134
Red Star exercises   135
Reflex deployment   85
Reforger exercises   113, 118
refuelling operations   113–14, 147–8
Republic
   F–84 Thunderjet   73, 84
   F–84E   76, 78, *79, 83*
   F–84F Thunderstreak   88, *92*, 96, 97, 98
   F–84G   82
   F–105 Thunderchief   20, *21*, 95, *95*, 103, *106*, 107, 108, 156
   P–47 Thunderbolt   *32*, 38, *39*, 40, 42, 43, 44, 47, 52, 64
   RF–84 Thunderflash   96, 98, *100*
Rhein Main air base   57, 67, *70, 82*, 82, 104, 110, 114, 122, 171, *171*
Rickenbacker, Captain Eddie   28, *29*
Ritchie, Captain Steve   *22*
Rockwell, B–1B   16
Rolling Thunder, Operation   20, 108, 156
Roosevelt, Franklin D.   29–30, *30*, 31, 33
Rota air base   166, 167

S

Sadat, Anwar   121, 144, 146
SALT (Strategic Arms Limitation) agreements   126, 143
Salty Nation exercise   164
SAM installations (Surface-to-Air Missiles)   156, 158
Sculthorpe air base   82, *86*, 113
Sembach air base   77, 104

Seventeenth (17th) Air Force   119, 122, 174–5
Seymour Johnson Air Force Base   103
Shemya Air Force Base   19
Side Looking Airborne Radar (SLAR)   107, 125
Sid Slimane air base   85
Sidewinder missiles   149, 150
Sikorsky, RH–53D Sea Stallion   144, *144*, 146
Six-Day War   119
Sixteenth (16th) Air Force   85, 174
Skydstrup air base   150
Smokey Hill Air Force Base   92
Soesterberg air base   108, 111, *170*, 172
Souda Bay marine base   170
Spangdahlem air base   77, 92, *95*, 106, 111, 113, *116*, 116, 129, 150, *152*, 167
Soviet Union
    aircraft current in service   22
    atomic weapons   74, 83
    Berlin blockade   62–72
    Berlin Wall   96–7
    Cuban crisis   103
    Dardanelles   60
    invasion of Afghanistan   143
    invasion of Czechoslovakia   *113*, 114
    invasion of Hungary   92
    and Lend-Lease   30, 54
    military aid to Egypt   89, 91
    and Poland   53–4
    post-war expansionism   56–7
    Vienna summit   95–6
    and Western air violations   77–80, 82, 104–7
Spaatz, General Carl   36, 47
Spad fighter aircraft   26, *26, 29*
Spain
    membership of NATO   168, 169
    US air bases   85, 103, 111–12, 168–9
Spangdahlem air base   158, *158*
Special Operations   18, 124
Spitfire   38, 40
spy planes *see* reconnaissance and surveillance
SS–20 missiles   135, 143, 153, 154
Stair Step deployment   98–9
Stalin, Joseph   54
standardization of aircraft *see* modernization programmes
Starkey deception plan   43
Stealth programme   22–3
Strategic Air Command (SAC)   16, 68, 74, 76, 84, 85, 93
Strategic Air Force   47, 53
Suez Canal crisis   89, 91
Sukhoi
    Su–22   161
    Su–25   22
    Su–27   22, 148
surveillance *see* reconnaissance and surveillance

Tactical Air Command (TAC)   12, 94
Tactical Airlift Wings (TAWs)   114, 124
Tactical Electronic Reconnaissance Systems (TERECs)   155
Tactical Nuclear Capability (NATO's)   84
Tactical Reconnaissance Wings (TRWs)   106, 155
tactical training *see* combat exercises; pilots' training
Tactical Wings   76–7
Takhli air base   *21*
Tegel air base   70, 72
Tegel airfield   70–1, 72
Tempelhof   68, 69, 70, *71*
TERCOM (Terrain Contour Matching) system   155
terrorist attacks on military installations   171, *171*
Thatcher, Margaret   163
Third (3rd) Air Force   173–4
Thirteenth (13th) Air Force   19
Tonapah test range   23
Torch invasion of North West Africa   36
Torrejon air base   95, 103, 111, 125, 168, 169, *169*
Total Force Strategy   22, 138
Toul-Rosieres air base   77, 92, 99, 110
transport of material and personnel   104
Trojan strategy   84
trucking missions   51
Truman, Harry S.   54, *54*, 57, 59, 76, *78*

Truman Doctrine   59
Tunner, General William   64, 66, 69
Tupolev
    Tu–16   83, *84*, 142
    Tu–95   83, 142, *142*
Turkey   59, 60, 112, 170
Tuschino air base   83
Twelfth (12th) Air Force   47
Twenty-first (21st) Air Force   18
Twenty-second (22nd) Air Force   18
Twenty-third (23rd) Air Force   18
Tyndall Air Force Base   13

U
U-boats
    attacked by Allied bombers   38
    attacks on Allied shipping   31, 36–7
United States Air Force (USAF)   9, 12
United States Army Air Force (USAAF)   12
US Air Forces in Europe (USAFE), origin of title   53
US Air Forces in the British Isles (USAFBI)   35
USS *Maddox*   20
U Tapao air base   20
Upper Heyford air base   84, 110, 114, 116, 125, 126, 152, 165

V
V–1   154
Vienna summit   95–6
Vietnam War   20, 115
Vittles, Operation *see* Berlin, airlift
Volkel air base   152

W
Waddington air base   68
Warsaw Pact
    air defense   156
    combined forces   21, 136
    establishment   89
Weinberger, Caspar   168–9
Wendling air base   *50*
West European Union (WEU)   87
West Germany
    membership of NATO   86, 87
    US air bases   111
Wheelus air base   101, 119
Wiesbaden air base   66, 67, *70*, 78, 105, 122, 125
William Tell defense exercise   13
Wilson, Thomas Woodrow   25
World War I
    demobilization   28
    Escadrille Americaine   25–6
    Escadrille Lafayette   26–7
    strategic role of aircraft   28, 29
    US combat aircraft   27, 28
    US declaration of war   25
    US neutrality   25
    volunteers   25, *27*
World War II
    British/US offensive strategy   31, 41
    demobilization   53
    deployment to Britain   35
    first all-US raid in Europe   36
    German surrender   52
    Lend-Lease Act   30
    Luftwaffe fighting strength   45
    preparations for invasion of Europe   49–50
    strategic bombing policy   33, 34–5
    US bombing missions   35–6, 37–44, 45, 46–7, 48–9, 50–1, 52
    US declaration of war   31
    US neutrality   30
Wright brothers   9
Wunsdorf air base   66

Y
Yalta conference   53
Yokota air base   20

Z
Zaragoza air base   103, 112, 125, 169
Zweibrücken air base   101, 122, 172